This book is for Tessa,
Matt's completely remarkable mum
and an inspiration to us all.

THE PLANT-BASED COOKBOOK

100 simple vegan recipes to make
every day delicious

Contents

Deliciously Ella
The Plant-based Cookbook

The last few years have been an incredible experience, a huge learning curve and, at times, an emotional roller coaster. In fact, I can't begin to explain just how unexpected the whole Deliciously Ella journey has been. When I first started writing my blog in 2012, I had no idea that it would engage the interest of so many people or end up becoming such a huge part of my life. I never thought that it would grow to the size it has and I definitely wouldn't have guessed that an interview I gave for my first book would be the catalyst for my introduction to Matt, my now husband, and kick-start a whirlwind romance that ultimately turned Deliciously Ella into a family business where Matt is our CEO, I'm the creative director and our dog, Austin, is king!

In this book I want to give you a glimpse into the Deliciously Ella world and share some of my personal insights from recent years, including how I turned a blog into a large community of people, bound together by a collective sense of values, purpose and passion. As well as my story, I want to share our plant-based philosophy and – of course – some very special recipes that I know you will enjoy making and eating.

I think it's worth saying now that while Deliciously Ella has grown and adapted, my ultimate aim has remained the same: to make fruits and vegetables more interesting and delicious, and inspire you to put them at the centre of your plate.

I'm excited to share the stories of our adventures, the lessons we've learnt (the good and the bad!), the advice we've been given and, best of all, the recipes that tell these tales. To me, the recipes that have developed over this period – from our kitchen, delis, pop-ups, festivals, dinners and supper clubs – are so much more than words on paper; they're little pieces of our journey, and together they form the building blocks that have made us who we are today. I can't wait for you to fall in love with them too.

Our journey

As many of you might know, I started Deliciously Ella in 2012 as a way of recording my own experiments in the kitchen as I learnt to cook and looked for ways to manage an illness that had affected my autonomic nervous system and had me largely bed-bound. Since then, I feel that both Deliciously Ella and I as a collective have been through two stages of growth and development.

Phase one was completely organic and unexpected as Deliciously Ella evolved from a personal diary that I initially wrote in my student kitchen and then my parents' kitchen, to a small but strong community on social media. From day one I spent a huge amount of time getting to know my audience and connecting with as many people as possible, and as that community grew both my readers and I wanted to take that connection from the online space into something more tangible. So I hired a small team who worked with me in my flat to organise supper clubs, talks and workshops. The next step was our app and on the back of that came my first book deal, which changed everything.

Somehow my first book caught a moment: our community had such a connection to the journey of Deliciously Ella that they all wanted to hear more. A week or so before the book was due to be published, orders went through the roof – to the point where my publisher rang me to let me know that they'd run out of books and were reprinting it across six different printers to keep up with demand! Nothing has ever surprised me more, and I can't tell you how surreal it felt watching it sit at the top of the bestseller chart. Up until this point in my Deliciously Ella journey, most people were still asking me when I was going to go and find a real job!

It was an amazing moment in my life and something for which I'll be forever grateful. Ultimately, Deliciously Ella has shaped everything I do and has led me on the most wonderful path, but at the time I wasn't ready for the intensity with which my career took off or the attention that I started to receive. If you remember, I got ill halfway through my time at university,

Deliciously Ella has shaped everything
I do and has led me
on the most wonderful path.

so I'd never had a proper job before, which meant I was pretty clueless on the professional front, and on a personal level I was still struggling to rebuild my self-confidence and self-esteem after my illness had taken such a hammer to them both. I'd spent most of the previous few years on my own watching other people's lives unfold via Facebook and I had a very negative view of myself and my self-worth, so suddenly operating in the public space was pretty terrifying. I had a few periods where I felt so far outside my comfort zone and incredibly vulnerable, which created a sense of real anxiety. I ran with it to a point, and tried to be a 'yes person', but rather than me making proactive decisions, everything I did was very reaction-led, as I just wasn't sure what to do, where to take Deliciously Ella next or how to create something meaningful for the community that supported me. Just as I started questioning everything, I was introduced to Matt, and that turned my world upside down in so many different ways.

Matt got in touch with me via our parents, who used to work together (we're basically an arranged marriage!), after reading an interview I gave about my new book. He'd been working on a social impact food and farming business in Sierra Leone, which had been put on hold due to the Ebola crisis, so he was looking for his next project and was interested in whether there was any connection between what we were doing. We met and that was that really. I went back to the girls at home and told them that I was in love. Luckily he felt the same, and things were turbocharged from there – he asked me out, we essentially moved in together after a week, got a dog two months later, got engaged four months after that, and were married a year later! Most people thought we were mad, some people thought I was joking about our engagement and a couple of people on social media even wrote to me to tell me that it would never last because I was rushing into it, but it is without a doubt the best decision I've ever made. The funny thing is that we tell everyone we started working together because we felt our complementary skills would help us build Deliciously Ella so much more successfully, but really, we just wanted an excuse to hang out together every day!

In some senses, it's ironic that we went into business together so that we could spend all of our time together as we now seem to spend all of it working, but there's something really special about creating a life that is based so intensely on a sense of partnership. We walk to the office together every day with Austin, usually stopping at the deli for breakfast. It's my favourite part of the day and a real little family ritual. Matt is the person that I turn to for advice on everything and he has helped me find the confidence to overcome that initial sense of vulnerability I felt about growing Deliciously Ella and expanding our community.

I just wasn't sure what to do, where to take Deliciously Ella next or how to create something meaningful for the community.

Creating this life together has been the greatest joy in my own life, and what's so interesting is the serendipity of the timing: us meeting and starting working together was the catalyst to kick-start the second phase of Deliciously Ella.

Phase two of Deliciously Ella was when it stopped being just about my personal journey, and instead became about a sense of community, a shared belief and ways to expand, introduce and make plant-based eating more aspirational and delicious. Over time, Deliciously Ella has come to represent that collective feeling and become part of the fast-growing movement celebrating plant-based living, rather than being solely a personal reflection.

It's the community that shapes and guides the way we think, what we work on and ultimately helps us define our wider goals.

At the same time, we stopped being reactive and started being (very!) proactive. We began hiring experts, building the team that we have today and making proper business plans. Since then, I've learnt more than I ever thought I could. We've made a huge number of mistakes (more than I can begin to count) and been challenged to the point of breaking, but we've grown massively – both as people and as a company. I'm proud to say we've launched multiple products into major supermarkets around the country, published three more books, which have now been translated into over 20 languages, opened delis in London, organised several pop-ups at festivals across the country, created two natural beauty lines with Neal's Yard Remedies, and so much more.

When I was thinking about what would come next, this book was at the top of my list. I wanted to bring together our best recipes and give you a better insight into our journey, who we are today and, most importantly, convey what Deliciously Ella has come to stand for. First and foremost it is about so much more than just me – despite my name being in the company name! Internally the business comprises more than 40 people, who together breathe life and love into everything we do, and we would never have got to where we are today without them. Externally, it's the community that supports us and what we do, the millions of people that follow us online and the loyal readers that come to our events, read our books, eat our products and come to see us at the deli. It's this community that shapes and guides the way we think, what we work on and ultimately helps us define our wider goals. We're a community-led company and we want to be guided by the heart of that – ultimately that's why we exist, to be a useful resource and tool for all of you.

What we believe

Over the last few years we've seen a huge rise in the popularity of healthy eating, which at its core is a great thing, but at times I think the conversation surrounding it has become too complex and polarising, making eating a bit better seem alienating for some. There has been so much debate around good food, bad food, healthy food, unhealthy food, clean food, dirty food, what we should be eating and what we shouldn't be eating, and to be honest it's all got a little confusing.

When I first started the Deliciously Ella blog, I was writing solely for myself and the (very!) few people that read it. I spent all of my time learning to cook, trying new recipes and reading as much as I could about food, which I shared on my blog. Truth be told, I found it quite confusing – there were so many different people saying slightly different things – and I found it challenging to navigate the right path for me, a scenario that I'm sure lots of us have experienced. I got swept up in the benefits of 'superfoods' and adopted what was, on reflection, a pretty regimented approach. But remember I was really unwell at that point and felt that I had to do everything and anything to try and get better. Something in my approach worked, as I was gradually able to gain control of most of my symptoms, but I think that was the combination of eating better, working closely with a nutritionist, the exercise programme my doctors put me on and a general overhaul of my student lifestyle – my diet played a large role but not the sole role.

As Deliciously Ella took off and I started to manage my condition much more successfully, I realised three things. Firstly, that I was not able to keep up the rigidity of the diet working in the way that I was – it was simply too time-consuming and required ingredients that weren't easily accessible, so something would have to shift to some extent. Secondly, that I was on top of the symptoms and therefore I could relax a little and find an approach that allowed me to continue to enjoy the plant-based food I'd fallen in love with but also allow me to do so alongside a pretty hectic lifestyle.

OUR
Philosophy

1. Eat Real Food!
2. Enjoy every mouthful, food is fun!
3. Buy food with thought, EAT WITH CARE!
4. Focus mostly on plants!
5. Eat organic when possible
6. DON'T WASTE! Share or keep for later
7. Find balance, don't diet!
8. Eat a rainbow everyday
9. Don't eat anything that your great grandmother would'nt recognise as food!
10. Listen to your body, your body knows BEST

Thirdly, that I was now talking to a much wider audience and Deliciously Ella had, in many ways unintentionally, become a resource for them, and what we were doing needed to reflect that. The more I learnt, the more I also appreciated that we all have to do what works best for us individually, because – as with anything in life – there is no one-size-fits-all. I realised how important it is to find the balance that suits and satisfies us each physically and mentally, and that taking anything to an extreme isn't a sustainable approach – whatever you do has to be genuinely enjoyable for the long term. It's inevitable that our balance will also shift and evolve week on week, month on month, year on year, depending on what else is happening in our lives.

Recent studies show that just 27% of the UK population is eating their five-a-day, let alone their ten-a-day.

These realisations, alongside a growing interest in the environmental and ethical side of plant-based living, have moved Deliciously Ella from that personal exploration to a resource for eating better and celebrating plants, and while I fully believe in finding your own balance I also believe that if we're ever going to get people eating their five-a-day, let alone their ten-a-day, then something is going to have to change. Recent studies show that just 27% of the UK population get their five-a-day, so somehow we've got to make broccoli, cauliflower and lentils a little more appealing! To do that, I think that we have to change two things: the first is the way we think about these foods – we need to show that eating a bit better doesn't have to be expensive, niche or inaccessible. And the second is the way we cook them: we need to show how to make fruits and vegetables as delicious as they can possibly be. It's not about becoming vegan or vegetarian, cutting your favourite foods from your diet or feeling restricted, it's simply about finding ways to enjoy more plants so that you genuinely want to incorporate them into your week in a way that works for you.

My biggest frustration with any of the criticism and commentary that is sometimes thrown our way is the suggestion that we put the concept of 'healthy' in the diet box, which is not a space to which I believe eating better belongs. I think categorising healthy eating alongside the likes of an Atkins or Dukan diet is what makes it appear restrictive and regimented. I really believe that 'healthy' has no specific definition, it has no rules or regulations and it should never come with a feeling of deprivation or play into the idea of a quick fix. It needs to celebrate abundance, doing delicious things with great ingredients and ultimately making people happier. I don't think we'll ever get near our five-a-day if we don't shift those negative views on healthy eating – I've met too many people who think eating a plant-based diet means you only eat lettuce leaves!

Eating healthily needs to celebrate abundance, creating delicious things with great ingredients and ultimately it needs to make people happier.

In the long run, I think showing people that eating well isn't about lettuce leaves and making veg more delicious is the most important element in shifting any negative preconceptions of healthy eating. I really don't think it's any more complicated than that – we need to make vegetables a little sexier and give them a little more love in our kitchens, as well as featuring them more prominently on our menus. That way we're going to start giving them the equal importance that we need them to have for the long-term health of our nation, and our planet. And this, in a nutshell, is the motivation behind Deliciously Ella.

DRINKS

Made with your choice of almond, coconut or oat mylk

HOT

Espresso	£2.50
Americano	£2.75
Latte	£3.25
Mocha	£3.50
Matcha Latte	£3.50
Turmeric Latte	£3.50
Hot Chocolate	£3.50
Organic Tea	£2.50

ICED

Iced Coffee	£3.50
Iced Matcha	£3.50

SMOOTHIES

Peanut Butter Protein £6.50
Banana, peanut butter, hemp protein, oats and oat mylk

Green Glow £6.50
Banana, spinach, almond butter and deep greens juice

Acai & Strawberry £6.50
Acai, strawberry, banana, blueberry, oats and coconut mylk

COLD PRESSED JUICES & MYLKS

330ml £4.75 / 500ml £6.95

Deep Greens Juice	Fruit Juice
Greens Juice	Cinnamon Mylk
Roots Juice	Chocolate Mylk

BANANA BREAD

With apple & berry compote and coconut yoghurt

£5.50

PORRIDGE WITH PEANUT BUTTER & BANANA
(made with oat mylk)

Creamy porridge with banana slices, peanut butter and maple syrup

£4.50

PORRIDGE WITH SEASONAL FRUIT COMPOTE
(made with oat mylk)

Creamy porridge with apple & berry compote, coconut yoghurt and coconut chips £4.95

PUDDING

With apple & berry compote and your choice of nutty or original granola

£5.50

BIRCHER MUESLI

With apple & berry compote and your choice of nut butter

£4.25

---

baked beans
avocado & sundried
tomato smash

£6.50

£3.50

GRANOLA FRUIT COMPO... & YOGHURT

With apple & berry compote a... coconut yoghurt

£4.25

What we've learnt so far

My first book was a very personal reflection of my health journey, what I'd learnt, what I'd tried and the foods that had helped me manage my illness. I was overwhelmed and humbled by the messages that I received by opening up about the struggles and challenges of this time, and when I thought about this book I wanted it to follow the same lines and be just as honest.

As I started writing this book I realised how much Deliciously Ella has changed my life. I know it might sound a little ridiculous but somehow my blog really has defined who I am and what I do in almost every way. It helped me get my health back under control, rebuild my self-esteem, find both a career and a passion, meet my husband, create a family business and generally steer me on a whole new path in life. It's also helped me build a strength and resilience that I never thought I could have and it's taught me so much, both professionally and about who I am as a person. So often people say to me, 'Did you ever expect to be where you are today?' and the only answer I can give is no, not in a million years. I was turning 20 when I got ill, 21 when I started blogging from my bed and 22 when I started sharing my meals on Instagram; at this point I had little to no ambition. I also wasn't sure if I'd ever be well enough to have a real job and I never thought writing a blog about my kitchen experiments would do much for shaping a career. Yet by 25 I was running a large team at work, had published three bestselling books, as well as a number one app, Matt and I had opened three delis, launched products in supermarkets across the country, I'd been on magazine covers and even been photographed by Mario Testino – who could have ever seen that coming?! I've certainly surprised myself more times than I can count and to be honest it all still feels pretty surreal.

Lots of people ask how Deliciously Ella got to this point, and I think the honest answer is that a lot of it has been luck, being in the right place at the right time; much of it has been a willingness to do whatever it takes and never take no for an answer, and the rest is down to a few other factors, which I want to talk about here. We've shared the journey with the community on social media but as we all know that can show more of a highlights reel and a snapshot of a moment, rather than a full account of what's happening, and I'm sure everything has all looked more polished and seamless than it's been in reality. There has definitely been a lot of organic growth and amazing opportunities, but equally it's been about making ourselves vulnerable and taking a terrifying leap into the unknown. We've put ourselves out there, been prepared to fail – and trust me we've failed and messed up more times than I could count – and we've had to be okay knowing that we will get criticised. Occasionally I've found that feeling unbelievably challenging and have felt uncomfortably vulnerable at times, but I'm learning to see those as passing feelings and instead just be grateful for the opportunities we have. I definitely believe that if you don't put yourself out there and challenge yourself to move out of your comfort zone every day, you'll never get to where you want to be.

We've put ourselves out there,
been prepared to fail – we've messed up
more times than I could count! –
and we've had to be okay with criticism.

While I learnt to embody that feeling of resilience, I simultaneously needed to learn everything I could about running a business as quickly as possible. I was still at university when I started Deliciously Ella, so it would be fair to say that I was missing pretty much all practical business know-how. I'll never forget talking to Matt when we first started working together. He was asking me relatively basic questions about my business and I just stared blankly back at him as if he was talking a foreign language. I didn't know what a P&L (profit and loss account) was, had never heard of a balance sheet, the only maths I could do was counting on my fingers and I had no idea how to calculate a margin. On the people side of things, I'd never been in a job interview before or had a boss, so I didn't really know where to start with running a team and I certainly didn't know how to manage one with much more experience and knowledge than me. I've tried to soak in everything I can over the last few years and have learnt a huge amount, but I still have a long way to go and am incredibly grateful for the constant support that our team provides. It's thanks to their brilliance that we've been able to drive this forward.

I've really enjoyed learning all the practical bits but my biggest take-home so far has been the importance of attitude and I really feel that a great outlook is a game changer. I went to a talk a few years ago where the speaker said that the one quality you need to create a successful business is optimism. Every other talk I'd been to had focused on the more obvious things – creating a great product, clever marketing, good margins and all the rest, but nothing had resonated with me more than this concept of unwavering optimism. The reality of starting your own business means there will be a lot of problems, a lot of unexpected crises and a lot of sleepless nights worrying about everything, some of it rational and some of it completely irrational. I'm a real worrier by nature and have a tendency to overthink everything, which isn't ideal when running a business and I definitely spent a lot of hours panicking and worrying at the beginning. I'll never forget sitting on the floor of the kitchen in our first deli crying and telling Matt that we couldn't leave for our own wedding after a series of disasters had unfolded. It was at this point that I realised my attitude needed to change; my worrying and constant desire to make everything perfect had gone too far and I had to start focusing on solutions, plus I also really needed to go to my own wedding! I've been working really hard on embracing that unwavering positivity and solution-solving attitude ever since. Going to yoga has really helped with that as it's calmed my mind more effectively than anything, and over time I've come to realise that nothing is as bad as it seems and even the worst issues get resolved. I still worry and we still have a lot of hurdles to overcome, but my sanity is definitely in a better place now!

My second biggest lesson when it came to attitude came from Matt. On his first day of work with Deliciously Ella he said, 'We need to be the dumbest people in this room.' I thought he sounded a little insane, but he could not have been more right. I'm the first to admit that I'm a stubborn person; I like doing things my own way and I always have an opinion on everything! I ran Deliciously Ella on my own at the beginning, it was an incredibly personal project and naturally I felt very protective of it. People saw me as 'Deliciously Ella' rather than Ella, founder of Deliciously Ella, and I knew that being so intrinsically connected to the brand and the name would make it hard for me to let people in and hand over part of the control to them. But as hesitant as I was, I knew that I could never take my passion and mission further without their expertise and advice, as I simply didn't have the knowledge or the confidence.

> On his first day of work with Deliciously Ella Matt said, 'We need to be the dumbest people in this room.' I thought he sounded a little insane, but he was right.

To go forward both Matt and I needed to acknowledge where our strengths lay and the areas in which we could help the business, but also where our weaknesses were and where they could potentially hold us back. My strengths lie in the brand side of things: the community engagement, the communication, the food and the general look and feel of everything. Matt had worked in finance and business development and had a real understanding of running a company, which is why he took on the CEO role – he's also a million times better at managing people than me! Neither of us had ever worked in the food or retail space though, so we prioritised finding a team with the expertise and experience that we lacked, learnt to take their advice and let them have real autonomy in their areas of the business.

Our team has been a crucial element of our journey and they make up a large part of the Deliciously Ella family, alongside the amazing community that has been kind enough to support us since day one. It's that community that I also believe has been pivotal in our journey. When I first started writing my blog I was lonely, I felt alienated from the people around me and was spending most of my time on my own at home. This also meant that I had a lot of time on my hands, so I replied to every single comment, query and question. I quickly realised how much I enjoyed connecting with everyone and how much I learnt from each person I engaged with, and that authentic connection has become the cornerstone of the Deliciously Ella community. I still personally respond to (almost) every tweet, Facebook, email and Instagram message. It's the first thing I do in the morning and the last thing I do at night; I check in on every bus ride, taxi journey and even when I'm walking down the street. It takes me three or four hours every day and I rarely, if ever, take a day off from it. It drives Matt a bit mad at times and a lot of people have told me that it's a total waste of my time, but I really believe it's been instrumental in our success. It's what created the sense of community and shared sense of purpose, it's what generated an audience for us and it's what keeps me so connected to the wider Deliciously Ella family every day – I love knowing what everyone is enjoying and cooking. It meant that we already had a large potential customer base when we transitioned into retail and supermarket products, which in turn meant that we had 50-metre queues the day after we opened our first deli, were able to secure Starbucks as a customer for our energy balls and, a year after launching our products, they were being stocked in thousands of stores across the UK from Waitrose, Sainsbury's, Whole Foods Market, Morrisons and Tesco to WHSmith, Boots and Holland & Barrett. What's more, initially we did it all without external investment, PR support or a marketing team – it was purely achieved through the direct connection with our readers. The support of that community means the world to us; we treasure it so much and taking care of it is always my number one priority. I'm always blown away by the people that take the time to come to our events, say hello in the deli and send lovely messages. I'm not sure they know how much we appreciate it but I promise we really do – you make our day every time! Hearing that you love one of our recipes, eat our granola for breakfast or treasure your copy of one of our books is unbelievable.

Our team has been a crucial element of our journey and they make up a large part of the Deliciously Ella family.

That being said, the comments aren't always positive and it's inevitable that there will be misunderstandings and some people aren't going to like everything we do. Accepting that we can't make everyone happy is something that I really struggle with – it's the thing that has got me down the most and it's the only thing that has ever prompted me to say, 'I quit'. However, I'm learning that there is an element of vulnerability for anyone starting their own business and that really intensifies if you choose to operate through the public lens, so you've got to find a way to accept it and move on. Now, when it comes to the negatives, I deal with them by dividing the criticism into two categories.

Deliciously Ella is a living, breathing collection
of people and every day we wake up
with a sense of purpose – to make eating well
easier and to spread our love of plants.

The first is constructive criticism which, although sometimes hard to hear, has been so important for us. It's helped us reassess what we're doing and ensure that we're doing everything as well as we can. It pushes us to do better and be better in every sense. Looking at our weaknesses has definitely helped us with our long-term goals and knowing that our audience will keep us in line is a great thing and helps us to uphold our key values, even when that is much harder to do! The second is the kind of criticism that I'm just learning to tune out, as it just brings me down and isn't constructive. It's when people write totally unnecessary personal comments telling me I've put on weight, that I look pregnant (when I'm definitely not!), that I have an annoying voice, that I am just generally irritating or that I rushed into my marriage so it won't last. I don't think there's a huge amount to gain by taking these types of comments on board, so I'm always looking for ways to ignore them!

I hope this has given you more of an insight into the human side of Deliciously Ella, and you can see that it is a living, breathing, mistake-making collection of people. Every day we wake up with a sense of purpose – to make eating well easier and to spread our love of plant power. Some days we do well, other days not so much, but each day we learn a huge amount and we can't wait to take this all further in the future.

These recipes embody every aspect of our journey – they've seen us through our highs and lows, and their delicious flavours have created a sense of happiness for us all. They are a true reflection of everything we've done in the last few years, and each one has a story of its own and represents a little piece of our adventure. I really hope you will enjoy reading about them and making them at home as much as we've enjoyed creating and sharing them.

A few notes before you get started

- We use medium-sized fruit and veg unless otherwise stated.

- Onions and garlic are assumed to be peeled unless we've suggested otherwise.

- We like to cook with sea salt, but feel free to use whatever you like best and adjust the levels to suit your taste. Where the recipe does specify a certain type (sea salt or table salt) it's because the flavour and/or texture will make a difference to the outcome of the recipe.

- For the cake recipes we recommend sticking to the tin sizes that we've specified to get the best results. If you double up the quantities or use a different-sized tin, the cake won't always cook all the way through.

- We've tried to suggest substitutions where possible, but by and large we do recommend sticking to the recipe given for the best results.

- We don't use any fancy equipment, but a blender and a food processor are pretty essential for making these recipes. We also use a spiraliser in one or two, but you could use a Y-shaped peeler or julienne peeler to the same effect.

Some of our common ingredients explained

ROASTED GARLIC

You'll find that some of our recipes suggest using roasted garlic. I know this might seem like extra work but cooking the garlic like this gives it a lovely sweetness, which adds a gentle mellow flavour to dishes rather than the sometimes harsher flavour of the raw cloves. We roast a batch of bulbs/cloves when we've got the oven on and keep them for the next time we're making a hummus, dip or falafel – they'll be fine stored in an airtight container in the fridge for up to a week.

To make them simply preheat the oven to 200°C (fan 180°C). Separate the cloves, peel them and place on a baking tray – you can bake them dry or use a little drizzle of olive oil. Roast for 10 minutes, then leave to cool before storing.

TOASTED NUTS AND SEEDS

As with the garlic, it may sound like extra work to toast your nuts and seeds but it really does bring out their flavour. It makes them crunchier too, which we love as it adds texture.

Preheat the oven to 200°C (fan 180°C). Place the nuts you are toasting on a baking tray in the oven for 5–10 minutes, until they go golden. We tend to cook flaked nuts for 5 minutes and whole nuts for 10 minutes.

APPLE CIDER VINEGAR

This is a key ingredient for us, both for dressings and salads to add tang, and in baking. The acidity of the cider vinegar helps make the batter fluffy and, because it's made from apples, it's sweeter than other vinegars. We also find it has a milder flavour, so your cake won't end up tasting like a salad but it will be a little lighter and fluffier.

ARROWROOT

Arrowroot is used as a thickener. We use it in baking mostly for things like glazes, although it can also be used as a way to thicken soups, stews, gravies and sauces. You can buy it online or in big supermarkets, or try using tapioca or cornstarch instead.

BUCKWHEAT/BROWN RICE/SPELT/PLAIN FLOUR

These are the four flours that we use most in our cooking, alongside polenta in things like our corn fritters and corn bread. The buckwheat and brown rice flours are gluten-free, but the spelt isn't – you can swap it for a plain white flour (we use a gluten-free one at the deli). Likewise, some people find the flavour of buckwheat flour to be strong and this can also be substituted for plain white flour.

CACAO BUTTER

Cacao butter is a pale-yellow fat that is extracted from the cocoa bean. We melt it down and mix it with other ingredients, then, as it cools, it sets and solidifies. It's great in things like our peanut butter cups for creating a thick chocolate layer.

BREAKFAST

The Deliciously Ella Diary
— *part 1*

The idea for our first deli came about after a walk Matt and I took in June 2015. We'd been talking about where to go for lunch and I was trying to persuade him that we should go to a raw vegan place because they made great kale salads and veggie sushi rolls, and he was keen to try a pizza spot. We talked a lot about how food can feel too black and white, either too healthy or not at all, and that we needed to make finding a middle ground much easier – a way of making eating our five-a-day more doable and delicious for everyone. And, just like that, we decided to go into business together and create that middle ground. We'd had so many requests from readers to open a space, which gave us an extra push and helped to boost our confidence in the idea. Both of us like to work fast and once we've set our sights on something there's no stopping us. So Matt quit his job in finance and we went from concept to reality between June and December of that year, diving headfirst into what turned out to be the hardest, funniest and most terrifying thing we've ever done.

It's tough to know where to start when describing how those first few months unfolded; I'm pretty sure I could fill a whole book with the stories, the funny moments and the lessons we learnt. I will restrain myself though, as I know you want to get on to the recipes, so I'll just share a little insight into their creation to give you the context in which they were brought to life and why they all have such special significance to us.

The first time we tried the recipes for our first deli turned out to be the single most hilarious, ridiculous moment of our journey to date. If I'm honest about it, it was the worst idea we've ever had and I'll never ever forget how much we both laughed and cried that week. A month before we opened we decided to test our menu. Our team of chefs was in place and we were impatient to get going, so we decided to do a week of deliveries in partnership with a delivery app called Quiqup. For some reason, we thought it would be best to run the operation out of our tiny one-room office on Bloomsbury Street, which is an incredibly busy, one-way street next to the British Museum in central London, with a lot of honking traffic and almost nowhere to stop to load delivery vans or bikes. The office was equipped with one small fridge and a team of three people, and in retrospect I'm sure we didn't have the right licence to run it out of there either. None of that deterred us though – we were totally sold on the idea being genius.

On the Monday, I made a big announcement across our social media channels that we were going live with lunch deliveries at 12pm and we all started refreshing our phones to watch the orders flood in. But nothing happened – not a single notification popped up. For the next 15 minutes no one said a word as we all processed the lack of orders, which led us to question whether this whole project may have been a huge mistake. Until we opened the door and saw a long line of drivers waiting to get their orders with more trying to park outside. It turned out we hadn't received the order details because we'd crashed the Quiqup app. Customers were going crazy for our Spiced peanut sweet potatoes (see page 96) and Charred broccoli and kohlrabi salad (see page 82). Relief quickly turned to blind panic as we realised we didn't have enough food, fridge space, packaging labels, general know-how, or hands, to man the whole thing. Matt rushed out to buy five more big fridges, which barely fitted through the door; we turned the desks we could upside down to make space, and the others became labelling stations. We begged friends to come and help us and didn't sleep for what felt like days, spending every minute handing out food boxes to the never-ending queue of drivers.

IT WAS NOTHING SHORT OF COMPLETELY AMAZING, AS IT SHOWED US THAT THERE WAS A DEMAND FOR WHAT WE WERE DOING AND WE COULD REALLY START RUNNING WITH OUR IDEAS

On the one hand it was total chaos, and I'm certain that any outside observer would have said we should quit while we were ahead as we evidently didn't have a clue, there was zero organisation and our stress levels were through the roof. On the other hand, however, it was nothing short of completely amazing, as it showed us that there was a demand for what we were doing and we could really start running with our ideas. Matt and I laughed so much that we cried almost every day watching the madness unfold and we were both so blown away by the love and support of the existing Deliciously Ella community. We probably should have learnt more from that experience and gone out to hire some knowledgeable managers instantly to help us open the first site on the basis that the demand would probably be more than we could deal with proficiently between us, but we were still very cautious about committing budgets we didn't have to anything and so we proceeded with blind optimism, a little naivety and huge excitement to the opening of our first deli.

We practically lived in the building site that would become our first deli on Seymour Place in Marylebone, London all of the following month, doing everything we could to get it open before Christmas. The day came on the 12th December; Matt and I had been there until at least midnight all of that week getting the last bits together and the decision to open the following day was a little impromptu. We still had more to finalise and we kept saying to each other again and again that we weren't ready, until we realised that we'd never be ready and we just needed to bite the bullet and get going – so we did. We didn't tell anyone online that we were open the first two days and just got lots of family and friends to come down and try it. I'm not really sure what they thought, to be honest; the set-up was still a little messy at our end but it was an incredibly proud weekend for us both. Things weren't perfect by any means, we still had so much to do and I was dealing with a big family drama at the same time, but we'd done it. Over the next few days word got out and suddenly we had 50-metre queues out the door! We didn't have any managers at this point – it was just me and Matt – so we were doing everything, from serving customers, to menu planning, ordering, creating rotas, cleaning the loos, doing the dishes and clearing tables. It was full on, to say the least. We implemented a system whereby I manned the tills and Matt cleaned tables, so that we could talk to each customer at the start and end of their visit to get as much feedback as possible. We worked 18 hours a day every day over those first six weeks or so, until our first manager Holly started. Holly instantly began implementing the systems that we sorely needed.

WE IMPLEMENTED A SYSTEM WHEREBY I MANNED THE TILLS AND MATT CLEANED TABLES, SO THAT WE COULD TALK TO EACH CUSTOMER AT THE START AND END OF THEIR VISIT

Just a few weeks in, we hit our first major hurdle when our head chef came to me during a manic lunch rush to say she was quitting and moving to

Barcelona. To say this was a blow is a massive understatement, and it was nearly the final straw. Having been working so hard to get the place up and running, I was suddenly terrified that we wouldn't be able to cope as there was just too much to do and I was gearing up to go away on a two-week book tour. I came home and told Matt, who was in bed with the flu and while I was crying and panicking he got straight on to finding the solution via LinkedIn. With our limited budget, we couldn't afford the premium LinkedIn subscription, so we trawled the site for candidates then hunted them down on their personal Facebook and Instagram pages. I'm a little embarrassed to think of people's reactions when they saw Matt commenting on personal photos of their families, asking them to call him. And we did have one moment where Matt emailed a potential candidate called Georgious – unfortunately autocorrect kicked in and he received a private message from Matt saying, 'Hey Gorgeous, I saw your profile online…' We still laugh about that mix-up and the general creepy desperation of the whole exercise, but it did work and eventually we got a brilliant team in place.

Over the next few pages you'll see the recipes that we've developed together over the last few years, starting with breakfast. Sharing these with you is our way of bringing our community to life, taking our food beyond the delis, into your home, and bringing us all a little closer. We hope you enjoy eating them as much as we all enjoyed creating them and we can't wait to hear what you think.

BUCKWHEAT PANCAKES WITH HOT CHOCOLATE SAUCE

We've had pancakes on the deli menu since day one and they're one of our most requested recipes, so I knew we had to share them. They've been through a few iterations, but this is my favourite. I love the subtle cinnamon flavour; it goes so well with the hot chocolate sauce.

**MAKES 10,
SERVES 3–4**

FOR THE PANCAKES
300ml coconut milk (from a carton)
140g buckwheat (or plain) flour
30g porridge oats
30g coconut oil, melted, plus more for frying
1 tablespoon coconut sugar
1 teaspoon baking powder
½ teaspoon ground cinnamon
pinch of sea salt

FOR THE CHOCOLATE SAUCE
280ml coconut milk (from a carton)
4 tablespoons cacao powder
70g coconut sugar
1 teaspoon arrowroot, dissolved in 2 teaspoons warm water (this thickens the mixture)
pinch of sea salt

TO SERVE
1 banana, sliced

Mix all the pancake ingredients together to form a smooth batter, then place the mix to one side and make the chocolate sauce.

Heat the sauce ingredients in a pan over a medium heat for 8–10 minutes, whisking until it turns into a smooth, creamy sauce.

Now cook the pancakes. Warm a tablespoon of coconut oil in a large frying pan over a medium heat. Once the pan is hot and the oil has melted, spoon in a heaped tablespoon of pancake batter, using a spatula to spread and shape the mix into a circle. Cook on one side for 4–5 minutes before flipping and cooking the other side for 2–3 minutes, until cooked through. Keep the cooked pancakes warm on a plate in a very low oven and repeat until all of the batter is finished.

Serve the pancakes warm with the sliced banana and a generous drizzle of the warm chocolate sauce.

TIP
If you want to make the pancakes more chocolatey, try removing the cinnamon and adding a heaped teaspoon of cacao powder to the batter, or make them fruity by adding some fresh berries to the batter before cooking.

APPLE AND BANANA SPELT MUFFINS

This is one of my favourite recipes in the book. We've become completely addicted to these muffins in our office and I've made them more times than I can count. They're adapted from a recipe shared by the lovely Steph, who ran the kitchen in Weighhouse Street for a period. She brought them into work one morning and we all loved them so much that we had to put them on the menu.

MAKES 12

2 red apples
3 ripe bananas, peeled
3½ tablespoons coconut milk
   (from a carton)
3 tablespoons coconut oil, melted

FOR THE DRY INGREDIENTS
230g spelt flour
200g coconut sugar
1 teaspoon bicarbonate of soda
½ teaspoon baking powder
pinch of ground cinnamon, plus
   extra for sprinkling

Preheat the oven to 200°C (fan 180°C). Line a 12-hole muffin tray with cases.

Core and peel one of the apples and cut it into small cubes. Leave to one side.

Mix the dry ingredients in a large bowl. In a separate bowl, mash the bananas until smooth, then add the milk and oil and stir together. Combine the wet and dry ingredients, then add the apple cubes and give everything another really good mix. Pour the mixture into the muffin cases.

Before baking, cut the remaining apple in half, core it, then cut each half into thin slices. Top each muffin with three slices and a sprinkle of cinnamon. Put the tray into the oven and bake for 25 minutes, until the muffins are golden and a knife inserted in the centre comes out clean. Once cooked, leave the muffins to cool in their tray for at least 10 minutes, to firm up, then transfer them to a wire rack to finish cooling or serve them warm out the tin.

TIP
Although spelt flour is best for this recipe, it also works with plain gluten-free flour. We tried other flours, including brown rice, buckwheat and coconut, but found they didn't create the right fluffiness. Also, note that the dough does look quite thick, so don't be surprised by that – it all comes together perfectly when baked.

GRANOLA

Original or
nutty granola with
your choice of
almond, coconut
or oat mylk
£3.50

GRANOLA
FRUIT COMPOTE
& YOGHURT

SIMPLE BLUEBERRY MUFFINS

These blueberry muffins are amazingly easy to make and the perfect addition to any brunch. We used to make them with a squeeze of lime juice and a sprinkling of zest, which was really delicious, so feel free to add those in if you want to add a little extra zing; if not then the recipe below is a real classic.

MAKES 12

100g blueberries
flaked almonds, to sprinkle
   on top (optional)

FOR THE DRY INGREDIENTS
400g spelt flour
100g coconut sugar
2 teaspoons baking powder
1 teaspoon bicarbonate of soda
1 tablespoon chia seeds
   (ground, if possible)
1 teaspoon mixed spice

FOR THE WET INGREDIENTS
100ml almond milk
170ml maple syrup
50ml rapeseed oil
1 teaspoon apple cider vinegar

Preheat the oven to 200°C (fan 180°C). Line a 12-hole muffin tray with cases.

Mix the dry ingredients in a large bowl. Once combined, add the wet ingredients. Mix until a batter has formed, then stir in the blueberries.

Pour the mixture into the muffin cases, sprinkle with the flaked almonds, if using, and bake for 25 minutes, until golden and a knife inserted in the centre comes out clean. Leave the muffins to cool in their tray for at least 10 minutes to firm up, then transfer them to a wire rack to finish cooling or serve them warm out the tin.

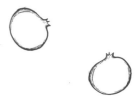

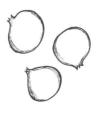

TIP
As with the Apple and banana muffins (see page 47), we found that spelt flour is best for this recipe. It also works with plain gluten-free flour but when we tried other flours, including brown rice, buckwheat and coconut, we found they didn't create the right fluffiness.

COURGETTE AND RED PEPPER MUFFINS

Finding savoury breakfasts and snacks can be a little tricky, so these are a really nice option for your morning. They're soft and spongy with lovely hints of cumin and paprika. If you'd like a hint of sweetness, you could try swapping the red pepper for some piquillo peppers from a jar; we used to do this and they're delicious.

MAKES 12

2 medium courgettes, peeled and grated
1 red Romano pepper (90g), deseeded and chopped into 5mm pieces
a few basil leaves, finely chopped, plus an extra handful to serve

FOR THE DRY INGREDIENTS
250g spelt flour
50g plain flour (we use a gluten-free one)
1 teaspoon baking powder
2 teaspoons bicarbonate of soda
1 teaspoon ground coriander
1 teaspoon ground cumin
1 teaspoon paprika
pinch of sea salt and pepper

FOR THE WET INGREDIENTS
280ml almond milk
65ml rapeseed oil
1 tablespoon apple cider vinegar

Preheat the oven to 220°C (fan 200°C). Line a 12-hole muffin tray with cases.

Start by mixing the dry ingredients in a large bowl. In a separate bowl, whisk the wet ingredients, then stir the grated courgette, pepper and basil into the wet mixture.

Combine the wet and dry ingredients, stirring well to ensure there are no lumps.

Pour the mixture into the muffin cases and bake in the oven for 25–30 minutes. Check them by seeing if a knife point inserted in the centre comes out clean and cook longer if needed. Leave the muffins to cool in their tray for at least 10 minutes to firm up, then transfer them to a wire rack to finish cooling or have them warm out the tin. Top with some basil leaves to serve.

TIP
We've been really specific with the weight of the red pepper as the water content makes a huge difference to the muffin texture. If you use more than we've suggested the mix will be too wet and may not cook through, so do stick to the 90g.

CRANBERRY AND RAISIN OAT BARS

These cranberry and raisin oat bars are an ideal breakfast for busy mornings, or make the most delicious mid-morning snack. The mix of ginger, nutmeg and cinnamon with the cranberries and raisins is so delicious, while the oats add chewiness to each bite.

MAKES 12

500g raisins
270g porridge oats
4 tablespoons coconut oil, melted
4 tablespoons rice syrup
2 teaspoons ground cinnamon
1 teaspoon grated nutmeg
1 teaspoon ground ginger
pinch of sea salt flakes
large handful of dried cranberries, about 60g

Preheat the oven to 190°C (fan 170°C). Line a 35 × 25cm baking tray with baking parchment.

Place three quarters of the raisins in a food processor, along with all the remaining ingredients except the cranberries. Pulse until the mixture comes together into a dough-like consistency. Add the cranberries and the rest of the raisins and give it another quick pulse to mix them through.

Transfer the mixture to the lined tray and bake in the oven for 20–25 minutes, until golden. Remove from the oven and leave to cool in their tray slightly before cutting into bars. Enjoy warm or at room temperature.

TIP
Make sure you do use rice syrup as the sweetener rather than maple syrup or sugar, as the thick liquid is what makes the bars stick together.

BANANA BREAKFAST LOAF

This banana bread is a real favourite – for us and for our customers. It's soft, sweet and full of lots of flavours from the cinnamon, almonds and banana, but if you want to make it more indulgent, try adding dark chocolate chips to the batter. I love this served with a dollop of our Apple and berry compote (see page 58), a scoop of coconut yoghurt and a drizzle of maple syrup.

MAKES 1 LOAF

430g ripe, peeled bananas
    (about 4 bananas)
20g pecans, halved

FOR THE DRY INGREDIENTS
150g ground almonds
125g buckwheat flour
1 teaspoon baking powder
1 teaspoon bicarbonate of soda
2 teaspoons ground cinnamon
pinch of salt

FOR THE WET INGREDIENTS
190ml maple syrup
55ml chickpea water (see tip below)
2 teaspoons apple cider vinegar

Preheat the oven to 190°C (fan 170°C). Line a 23 × 13 × 7cm loaf tin with baking parchment.

Put the bananas into a mixing bowl and mash with a fork until smooth and creamy – the riper they are the easier this will be. Next stir in the dry ingredients, mixing them well with the bananas. Then add the wet ingredients and stir until a smooth batter forms.

Spoon the mixture into the lined loaf tin, then sprinkle the pecan halves over the top evenly. Bake the loaf in the oven for 45–50 minutes or until a knife inserted into the middle comes out clean; if it doesn't leave the loaf in the oven a little longer. Once ready, leave to cool in the tin for 10 minutes to firm up, before transferring to a wire rack to cool to room temperature.

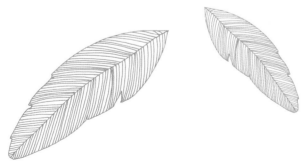

TIP
I know the chickpea water sounds strange, but it works in a similar way to egg whites in baking recipes, helping to create the perfect fluffiness.

APPLE AND BERRY COMPOTE

This is a staple in my life. I have it for breakfast most days, as it goes with just about everything, from porridge, granola and chia pudding to banana bread, toast with almond butter and cinnamon pancakes. It's also amazing eaten straight out the bowl!

SERVES 4

2 red apples, peeled, cored and roughly chopped
¼ teaspoon ground cinnamon
100g frozen raspberries (or any other frozen berries)
2 tablespoons maple syrup

Place the apples and cinnamon in a pan with a splash of water over a medium heat – the water will stop your pan burning, but don't add too much as the apples will release more liquid as they cook and you don't want the compote to be runny. Cook until soft – roughly 20–25 minutes, keeping an eye on the pan and stirring from time to time.

Once soft, stir in the frozen berries and maple syrup, cook for another 10–15 minutes, giving the compote mix a quick mash with the back of a fork every now and then, until it reaches your desired consistency – it will continue to thicken as it cools.

Once the compote is completely cool, you can store it in an airtight container in the fridge for 5–7 days.

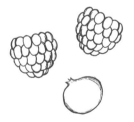

MAPLE AND WALNUT GRANOLA

We love granola; it's a must in the deli, the Deliciously Ella office and in our kitchen at home. I've been making variations on the recipe below for the last five years, but this is one of my all-time favourites. The mix of toasted walnuts, flaked almonds, coconut chips and sunflower seeds with vanilla, maple, orange and cinnamon is a dream and baking it will make your whole house smell amazing.

MAKES ABOUT 1KG

90g coconut oil
160ml maple syrup
grated zest of 1 orange, plus
    a squeeze of the juice
4 teaspoons ground cinnamon
1 vanilla pod, split lengthways
    and seeds scraped out
400g jumbo oats
70g sunflower seeds
50g pumpkin seeds
40g flaked almonds
40g walnuts
60g coconut chips
100g raisins

Preheat the oven to 160°C (fan 140°C). Line a large baking tray with baking parchment.

Heat the coconut oil and maple syrup over a low heat until melted. Remove the pan from the heat and add the orange juice, cinnamon and vanilla seeds.

Mix the rest of the ingredients – apart from the coconut chips and raisins – in a big bowl and pour in the oil and syrup mixture.

Spread the mixture evenly over the lined tray and bake for about 45 minutes, stirring every 5 minutes, until golden brown. Add the coconut chips for the last 10 minutes.

Remove the tray from oven and leave to cool. When the granola reaches room temperature, mix in the raisins. Store the granola in an airtight container – it will stay fresh for a couple of weeks.

TIP
Make sure the granola is completely cool before storing, otherwise it will go soggy really quickly.

COCONUT CHIA PUDDING

This is a super simple recipe that is perfect for busy mornings. I often make it the night before and leave it in the fridge, ready to grab and go as I rush out the door. I love the thick, creamy consistency of the pudding and normally serve it with our Apple and berry compote (see page 58) and a dollop of almond butter or a sprinkling of coconut chips.

SERVES 2

1 vanilla pod, split lengthways
    and seeds scraped out
    (or 1 teaspoon vanilla paste
    or powder)
230ml coconut milk (from
    a carton) or any other
    plant milk, such as
    almond, oat or rice, etc.
125g pure coconut yoghurt
65g chia seeds

Mix the vanilla seeds with the coconut milk and yoghurt. Slowly add the chia seeds, mixing as you add them to prevent lumps forming. Leave to thicken for about 10 minutes, mixing every few minutes to ensure the pudding thickens evenly. Store in the fridge.

RED BERRY CHIA PUDDING

This version of our simple coconut chia pudding has a deeper flavour, thanks to the blackberries, cardamom and lemon juice. It's also the most beautiful colour, making it the perfect addition to any brunch table. Try making this into little parfaits, with a layer of the chia at the bottom, followed by some yoghurt and some of our Maple and walnut granola (see page 61).

SERVES 2

100g frozen blackberries,
    or any other frozen berries
1 cardamom pod, split open
    and seeds ground
100ml coconut milk (from
    a carton) or any other
    plant milk, such as almond,
    oat or rice, etc.
2 tablespoons maple syrup
squeeze of lemon juice
50g chia seeds

Blitz the frozen blackberries, ground cardamom, coconut milk, maple syrup and lemon juice in a food processor until smooth, then pour into a bowl. If you don't have a food processor, mash with a fork.

Add the chia seeds, mixing as you go to prevent lumps forming. Leave to thicken for about 10 minutes, mixing every few minutes to ensure the pudding thickens evenly. Store in the fridge.

TIP
If you're leaving chia pudding overnight, you may want to add a little more milk in the morning to loosen it as it will continue to thicken in the fridge.

CORN FRITTERS WITH SMOKY BAKED BEANS AND AVO SMASH

These fritters are the basis of our go-to brunch and I can't begin to count the number of requests we've had for this recipe, so I hope you all enjoy making them at home. They're absolutely incredible with the avocado smash and our smoky baked beans, or else simply pile them high with garlicky sautéed tomatoes for a speedier option.

SERVES 4

FOR THE FRITTERS
1 × 300g tin of sweetcorn, drained
110g polenta
2 tablespoons buckwheat flour
2½ tablespoons plain flour
1 teaspoon bicarbonate of soda
2 tablespoons plain yoghurt
   (we use a pure coconut yoghurt)
140ml almond milk
1 red chilli, deseeded and sliced
handful of coriander or chives,
   chopped
salt and pepper

FOR THE SMOKY BAKED BEANS
olive oil
1 onion, sliced
2 garlic cloves, chopped
1 teaspoon ground cumin
1 teaspoon smoked paprika
½ teaspoon chilli powder
1 tablespoon tamari
1 teaspoon apple cider vinegar
1 × 400g tin of tomatoes
2 tablespoons maple syrup
1 × 400g tin of borlotti or red
   kidney beans, drained
1 tablespoon tomato purée
25g parsley, chopped

FOR THE AVO SMASH
2 large ripe avocados, peeled
   and stoned
juice of 1 lime
pinch of chilli flakes
1 tablespoon olive oil
handful of coriander,
   roughly chopped
75g sun-dried tomatoes,
   roughly chopped

If you're serving the fritters with the smash and beans, start by making the beans. Place a pan over a medium heat with a drizzle of olive oil. Once warm, add the onion and garlic and cook for 5–10 minutes, until soft. Add the spices and cook for a further minute, stirring constantly, then add the tamari, apple cider vinegar, tomatoes, maple syrup, beans and tomato purée. Bring the whole thing to the boil then reduce the temperature and leave to simmer for 15–20 minutes. Once the sauce has thickened, stir through the parsley and some salt and pepper. Keep warm over a low heat while you make the smash and fritters.

For the smash, place the avocado, lime juice, chilli, olive oil and some salt in a bowl and mash together using a fork. Stir through the coriander and sun-dried tomatoes.

To make the fritters, place two thirds of the sweetcorn in a food processor and blitz until smooth. Next place the polenta, flours, bicarb and a generous sprinkling of salt in a bowl and mix. Then add the yoghurt, blitzed sweetcorn and almond milk and give it a really good stir, until smooth. Stir through the chilli, coriander and remaining whole sweetcorn kernels.

Place a frying pan over a medium heat with a drizzle of olive oil. Once warm, spoon in one large tablespoon of the batter at a time and cook for 3–5 minutes, until golden and holding its shape, then flip over and cook the other side in the same way.

TIP
I always make extra beans, as they're delicious the next day and keep really well in the fridge for about 5 days or in the freezer for when you need a speedy breakfast/supper. Make sure you allow the leftovers to cool before putting in the fridge or freezer.

VEGAN SHAKSHUKA

This thick, rich tomato-based dish is perfect if you're looking for something warming and cosy. It's bursting with flavour and hits the spot every time. We make our version vegan-friendly, but if you'd like to adapt it and include eggs as per the traditional recipe then please do. If not we add dollops of thick coconut yoghurt in place of the eggs, which looks brilliant and adds a nice creamy element. As with the Smoky baked beans on page 65, this works really well for an easy lunch or supper too.

SERVES 2
AS A MAIN DISH,
4 AS A SIDE

FOR THE BASE
1 large onion, sliced
2 garlic cloves, sliced
olive oil
1 red pepper, deseeded and sliced
1 teaspoon ground coriander
1 teaspoon ground cumin
½ teaspoon paprika
½ teaspoon cayenne pepper
1 × 400g tin of plum tomatoes
2 tablespoons tomato purée
salt and pepper

TO SERVE
100g plain yoghurt (we use a pure
    coconut yoghurt)
handful of micro herbs or coriander

Place the onion and garlic in a pan over a medium heat with a little drizzle of olive oil, cover with a lid and sweat for 10-15 minutes, until soft.

Add the red pepper and spices and cook for a further two minutes. Then add the tomatoes, tomato purée, 200ml water, and some salt and pepper. Bring everything to the boil before reducing the temperature and leaving to simmer for about 20–25 minutes until thick and rich.

Serve with a few dollops of yoghurt on top and a sprinkle of chopped herbs.

TIP
This makes a brilliant pasta sauce too, so make extra and store it in the fridge for another day. Simply warm it up in a pan and stir through your cooked pasta.

OUR SALADS

The Deliciously Ella Diary
— *part 2*

As we go into the next section of recipes I wanted to dive a little further into our story, sharing how we grew Deliciously Ella during the next phase, moving away from the slightly experimental approach at Seymour Place to a more professional, although still pretty chaotic, one. It was a period during which we opened our next two sites, fed thousands of people at our first big festival and our first products landed on supermarket shelves. Throughout this time, we created the majority of the recipes you'll find on the next few pages, and they worked wonders in terms of helping to sustain us during crazy busy periods, persuading our future landlords to give us the sites we so wanted and swaying our internal team to come and join us. Food really does bring people together!

Within weeks of opening, Seymour Place was bursting at the seams. It was a beautiful space but it was small and relatively narrow upstairs (which is why the rent was affordable!). We knew that we had to get moving on our next space if we wanted to keep our customers happy, so Matt got back on the property hunt and quickly fell in love with a site on Weighhouse Street. We became a little obsessed with the site, loving the beautiful brick building, the big windows that flood the space with natural light and the peaceful feeling on the road, which is even more amazing considering it's only 50 metres or so from the bustle of Oxford Street. We hustled hard against an array of strong competition who outbid us time and time again but eventually won the landlords over with our food.

Although Weighhouse was bigger we were conscious that many of our readers weren't able to reach us on a daily basis so we started to look at ways in which we could spread our love of plants a little wider and bring what we were doing to everyone. After a lot of debate, we decided against rolling the delis out as a chain at this point, as we felt that we wouldn't necessarily be able to get the quality we wanted or the personal touch that was so important to both of us, and instead we started looking at bringing our recipes to supermarket shelves so that we could reach our wider community. We quickly realised we would need an expert team for this as, unlike the delis, we didn't think we could learn as we went along. I have no idea how we ended up with the talented group of people we have now, not least our first hire and current managing director, Dan. To this day I don't know how we persuaded him to take the leap and join us, leaving behind an amazing, stable job to head up a products department that had no products and no concrete plans – all we had at this point was one tiny site, lots of dreams and a growing sense of ambition. We threw him in at the deep end; he started in May and we launched on the 1st August so it was all systems go from day one, finding the right branding agency and packaging materials, talking to stockists and finding the right partners to work with.

> WE STARTED TO LOOK AT WAYS IN WHICH WE COULD SPREAD OUR LOVE OF PLANTS A LITTLE WIDER AND BRING WHAT WE WERE DOING TO READERS WHO COULDN'T REACH THE DELI

One of the qualities that Matt brings to the table every day is a phenomenal sense of confidence: he has no fear of putting himself out there and is happy to approach anyone on any subject. I was nervous about approaching stockists, whereas he was very assertive and used LinkedIn to hunt down the right buyers. One of my favourite moments was with Starbucks. I didn't think he should contact them on the assumption that a company like that

would never stock something by a small little family start-up, but Matt had other ideas. He found the MD on LinkedIn and sent emails to about 20 different variations on his name, hoping that one would get through – and it did. We heard back from him the next day and he called us in for a meeting. I was really nervous beforehand and was prepared to be laughed out of the

room, but it couldn't have gone better and they told us there and then that they wanted to stock our energy balls. Matt, Dan and I all tried to act really cool at this point but the second we got in the lift to leave we started screaming and jumping up and down. It was the most surreal moment; we'd just secured them as our second ever stockist and our products were about to be displayed at all their till points in their UK shops.

They called us the following day to say they wanted us to be in within six weeks, which meant we had to move fast. We said yes very enthusiastically and then started freaking out the second the phone went down. The issue was twofold: one, we weren't prepared for such big volumes in terms of packaging, ingredient supply, etc., and two, we were on our way to Wilderness Festival to run a pop-up deli, which meant that our office was a tent in the middle of a field with limited phone signal and a lot of noise! We didn't want to let on that we were at a festival and tried our best to create little soundproofed areas to talk to them from while trying to manage what turned out to be the craziest weekend we've ever had for the deli. I know some of our readers think we sold out by selling into Starbucks, but for us it was exactly what we wanted – to make plant-based, natural foods accessible in the mainstream.

AT WILDERNESS WE SERVED 1.5 METRIC TONS OF FOOD OVER THREE DAYS, WITH OVER 50 KILOS OF AVOCADO TOAST FLYING OUT OUR TENT WITHIN THE FIRST TWO HOURS

At Wilderness we served 1.5 metric tons of food over three days, with over 50 kilos of avocado toast flying out our tent within the first two hours. To say it was madness is an understatement. I couldn't help but laugh when people came in upset that there was no more avo toast available as I tried to explain that we just couldn't have foreseen needing more than 50 kilos of avocado that morning! We were also hosting four-course banquets with 80 people each evening and a tea with Neal's Yard Remedies to mark the launch of our skincare line that we'd created with them. It was one of the most memorable moments in our career, sitting cross-legged under a table in our makeshift kitchen trying to sound professional and under control on the phone to Starbucks as people were frantically blending smoothies next to us, looking for more ripe avocados, and every other second we were calling our partner begging for more capacity for the energy ball production, while in the background wild ravers were covered in glitter and dancing. We all looked a little shell-shocked when we left on the Monday, full of great memories and ready to get the energy balls out into the world.

The energy balls launched to much success in Whole Foods Market, Waitrose, Selfridges, Planet Organic and Starbucks, and we started the fit-out for Weighhouse, which had been massively delayed due to building issues. We were meant to open at the end of August and by early November we still weren't trading and things were getting tight financially; it was one of the scarier moments to date and a point at which we definitely got close to going out of business. The delays meant that the finish was not up to scratch, but we were desperate to get the place open. Matt and I had plans to celebrate our six-month wedding anniversary but as we realised the extent to which things had gone wrong and that we were still no closer to being finished, all plans were cancelled and we spent a romantic weekend camped out in a freezing cold building site. I remember sitting in the dark at two in the morning on the Friday night debating

what to do, and in the end, we decided the way forward was to paint the whole place white over the weekend to remedy the decorating disasters and just get the doors open so that the site didn't bring down the rest of the business. After we'd done it, Matt said the basement looked like a hospital waiting room. I was more optimistic and tried to fill it with plants, but it wasn't great. That said, at least we had customers in there at last and we had hopefully avoided going under. Six months later we had the budget to rectify the stark white look and it's now a lovely combination of dusty pink and navy blue with white marble table tops and (still!) lots of plants.

Luckily for us the food helped the place come to life and all the colourful dishes you'll see in this chapter helped to give it a warm, inviting feel. To me these dishes signify who we are and what our message is: that plants are delicious, that plant-based food is vibrant and abundant, and that eating healthily never needs to involve soggy lettuce or carrot sticks!

ASIAN-STYLE BROCCOLI AND BOK CHOY

This was one of our most popular dishes ever and is a nice, simple way to celebrate broccoli. The tamari, maple, sesame and chilli dressing adds great flavour to each bite, while the aubergine, bok choy and coriander add a great mix of colours and textures. We eat this as a side with just about everything – it's delicious with the Black rice, sweet potato and orange salad with toasted almonds and the Harissa-roasted aubergines (see pages 78 and 108).

SERVES 4 AS A SIDE

1 aubergine, cut into bite-sized
    pieces no bigger than 2.5cm
olive oil
2 bok choy, halved and sliced
600g Tenderstem broccoli
1 tablespoon sesame seeds
handful of coriander,
    roughly chopped
salt and pepper

FOR THE DRESSING
2 tablespoons sesame oil
1 tablespoon maple syrup
1 tablespoon tamari
pinch of chilli flakes

Preheat the oven to 240°C (fan 220°C).

Place the aubergine in a baking tray with a good drizzle of olive oil and some salt and pepper. Roast in the oven for 40–45 minutes.

While the aubergine is in the oven, place the bok choy and broccoli in a baking tray with a drizzle of olive oil and some salt and pepper, and give them a good mix. Add the tray to the oven for the final 10 minutes of the aubergine's cooking time.

Once the aubergine has turned golden and soft, and the broccoli and bok choy are tender and starting to char around the edges, remove the trays from the oven and leave to cool.

Next, make the dressing by simply mixing the ingredients together until smooth and season it with salt and pepper. Once the veg reaches room temperature, toss it with the sesame seeds, coriander and the dressing.

TIP
Tenderstem broccoli works really well in this salad, but broccoli florets are good too. Likewise, if you can't find any bok choy you can leave this out – just add a little more broccoli.

COURGETTE, CELERIAC AND PEANUT NOODLES

This is a brilliantly simple dish. It takes just 10 minutes or so from start to finish, and there's almost no washing up. It works well as a bed under a main dish, or as a light side. I love the creamy peanut butter and sesame dressing, the crunchy bite of peanuts and sesame seeds plus the fresh basil. The salad is best served immediately, as the salt will cause the courgettes to leak water, which can make it a bit soggy if left too long. If it does sit, simply stir the noodles to mix the excess water in with the dressing.

SERVES 4 AS A SIDE

1 large courgette, spiralised into
    noodles (or see tip below)
½ celeriac, peeled and spiralised
    into noodles (or see tip below)
handful of peanuts, about 30g,
    roughly chopped
handful of fresh basil,
    roughly chopped
1 tablespoon sesame seeds
salt and pepper

FOR THE DRESSING
1½ tablespoons smooth
    peanut butter
1 tablespoon sesame oil
1 teaspoon apple cider vinegar
juice of ½ lemon
pinch of chilli flakes (adjust
    to your taste)

Place the spiralised noodles in a large mixing bowl. Add the peanuts, basil and sesame seeds with some salt and pepper and give everything a good mix.

Next make the dressing by whisking all the ingredients in a bowl until smooth. Pour the dressing over the noodles and mix together before serving.

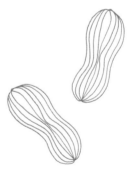

TIP
When it comes to making the noodles, don't worry if you don't have a spiraliser – you can use a grater, mandolin or julienne peeler to make thin strips of the veg instead.

BLACK RICE, SWEET POTATO AND ORANGE SALAD WITH TOASTED ALMONDS

This is one of my favourite recipes. The tender bites of sweet potato with the rich black rice, roasted aubergine, toasted almonds and coriander taste so good together, especially tossed with the sweet orange dressing. I love this served hot with a dollop of our Smoky aubergine dip and our Whole baked cauliflower (see pages 140 and 111).

SERVES 2
AS A MAIN DISH,
4 AS A SIDE

200g black rice, rinsed
1 aubergine, cut into bite-sized
    chunks no bigger than 2.5cm
olive oil
2 medium sweet potatoes,
    peeled and cut into
    bite-sized chunks no
    bigger than 2.5cm
80g flaked almonds, toasted
1 orange, peeled and cut into
    segments (optional)
pinch of chilli flakes
25g coriander, roughly chopped
salt and pepper

FOR THE DRESSING
2 tablespoons olive oil
juice of 2 oranges and the
    grated zest of 1 (adjust
    this to your taste –
    if you don't love strong
    orange flavours, halve
    the quantities of each)
1 tablespoon maple syrup

Preheat the oven to 240°C (fan 220°C).

Place the black rice in a pan, cover with water, bring to the boil then reduce to a simmer and cook over a medium heat for 40–45 minutes or until cooked to your liking. Drain and remove from the heat.

While the rice is cooking, place the aubergine in a large baking tray and mix with a drizzle of olive oil and some salt and pepper. Roast for 10–15 minutes. Once the aubergine has been cooking for 10 minutes, mix in the sweet potato chunks then put the tray back into the oven for another 30 minutes.

Once cooked, remove the aubergines and sweet potatoes from the oven and mix them with the rice, almonds, orange segments, if using, and chilli flakes. Mix the dressing ingredients together with some salt and pepper and pour over the salad, stirring well, then sprinkle over the chopped coriander.

TIPS

If you're making this salad in the summer, it's delicious to enjoy with pieces of orange mixed through to make it taste fresh and look even more vibrant.

Grate some of the zest from the other orange on top of the salad before serving – it looks beautiful! We like this served hot, straight from the pan, but it's great as a cool salad too. If there are any leftovers, leave them to cool before storing in an airtight container for a few days – we don't recommend reheating this.

ROAST SQUASH, SPRING ONION AND MIXED RICE SALAD

I love how fresh this dish tastes, it's one of my summer go-tos. The mix of spring onions, parsley and peppers with the tangy apple cider, lemon and pomegranate dressing gives each bite a real zest, while the mixed rice and butternut squash bring it all together. It's delicious with our Classic hummus (see page 136) and also makes a brilliant desk lunch.

**SERVES 2
AS A MAIN DISH,
4 AS A SIDE**

50g wild rice, rinsed
100g brown rice, rinsed
1 small butternut squash, peeled, deseeded and cut into bite-sized pieces no bigger than 2.5cm
olive oil
1 yellow pepper, deseeded and cut into bite-sized pieces no bigger than 2.5cm
1 red pepper, deseeded and cut into bite-sized pieces no bigger than 2.5cm
4 spring onions, thinly sliced
10g parsley, roughly chopped
salt and pepper

FOR THE DRESSING
2 tablespoons olive oil
1 tablespoon apple cider vinegar
1 tablespoon pomegranate molasses
squeeze of lemon juice

Preheat the oven to 200°C (fan 180°C).

Place the wild and brown rice in a pan, cover with water, bring to the boil then reduce the heat to a simmer and cook over a medium heat for 40–45 minutes until cooked through. Drain and leave to one side to cool to room temperature for up to an hour, then place in the fridge until ready to use.

While the rice is cooking, place the butternut squash in a baking tray with a drizzle of olive oil and some salt and pepper, and roast for 40–45 minutes or until cooked through.

While the squash roasts, make the dressing by whisking the ingredients until smooth.

Once the squash is cooked, place all the salad ingredients in a large bowl, add the dressing and mix well before serving.

TIP
You don't have to use butternut squash in this recipe, you can use any squash that is in season – acorn, carnival, onion and spaghetti squash all work well.

CHARRED BROCCOLI AND KOHLRABI SALAD

The creamy almond and sesame dressing in this salad is so good – I use it all the time and find it instantly brings everything to life. The mix of tender kohlrabi slices with roasted broccoli, garlic and chilli is delicious, especially with the black beans.

**SERVES 2
AS A MAIN DISH,
4 AS A SIDE**

2 kohlrabi, peeled, chopped and
    cut into thin slices (celeriac
    is a great swap too)
olive oil
300g Tenderstem broccoli
    or 1 large head of broccoli,
    chopped into florets
3 garlic cloves, chopped
2 red chillies, deseeded and sliced
1 × 400g tin of black beans,
    drained and rinsed
salt and pepper

FOR THE DRESSING
2 tablespoons almond butter
2 tablespoons sesame oil
2 garlic cloves, peeled and
    chopped
1 teaspoon lemon juice

TO SERVE
handful of almonds, toasted (see
    page 35) and roughly chopped

Preheat the oven to 220°C (fan 200°C).

Place the kohlrabi in a baking tray. Drizzle with olive oil, season with salt and pepper and roast for 25 minutes. Add the broccoli, garlic and chilli to the tray, then place it back in the oven for another 10 minutes. Once everything is cooked, remove from the oven and leave to cool.

Put the black beans into a big bowl along with the rest of the salad ingredients.

Stir the dressing ingredients together with some salt and pepper and pour over the salad, mixing well. Serve with a sprinkling of almonds on the top.

TIP
If you can't find kohlrabi you can roast celeriac in the same way, or skip it altogether and double the quantity of broccoli.

CREAMY CAULIFLOWER AND CHICKPEA SALAD

This is one of my favourite salads we've shared so far – I love the creamy yoghurt dressing with the fresh tarragon and parsley. Using Romanesco broccoli and purple cauliflower makes it look so beautiful too. I think this tastes fantastic on its own, but it's also great with a simple quinoa salad or as part of a salad spread.

**SERVES 4
AS A MAIN DISH,
8 AS A SIDE**

1 Romanesco broccoli,
    cut into florets
1 small cauliflower, cut
    into florets
1 small purple cauliflower,
    cut into florets
olive oil
150g button mushrooms,
    cut into quarters
1 × 400g tin of chickpeas,
    drained and rinsed
10g fresh parsley, roughly
    chopped, plus an extra
    handful to serve
handful of fresh tarragon,
    about 5g, roughly chopped
salt and pepper

FOR THE DRESSING
2 generous tablespoons plain
    yoghurt (we use a pure
    coconut yoghurt)
2 tablespoons olive oil
1 garlic clove, thinly sliced
1 tablespoon apple cider vinegar
1 tablespoon maple syrup

TO SERVE
large handful of pine nuts,
    about 40g

Preheat the oven to 240°C (fan 220°C).

Place the broccoli and cauliflower florets in a large baking tray, drizzle with olive oil, and add salt and pepper. Add the mushrooms and chickpeas, mix and place in the oven for 10–15 minutes, until the broccoli is charred. Once cooked, remove from the oven and leave to cool.

Make the dressing by whisking the ingredients until smooth. Lightly toast the pine nuts in a dry frying pan over a medium heat until golden. It takes around 2 minutes but be sure to keep tossing them as they burn easily – tip them out the pan to stop the toasting.

Once the veg is cool, mix with the parsley and tarragon. Stir the dressing through the salad, before sprinkling with the pine nuts and the extra parsley.

TIP
If you can't find the different types of cauliflower in this recipe, you can just use 2–3 regular cauliflowers.

CRUNCHY ASPARAGUS, CARROT AND HAZELNUT SALAD

If you're looking for a fresh spring salad this is fantastic. It's light and full of veg with the asparagus, carrots, peas and radishes, while the toasted hazelnuts add a great crunch and the mint keeps it tasting fresh.

**SERVES 4
AS A MAIN DISH,
8 AS A SIDE**

250g baby carrots, sliced lengthways, or 4 medium carrots, cut into batons
1 teaspoon chilli powder
1 teaspoon ground cumin
1 teaspoon smoked paprika
1 teaspoon ground coriander
olive oil
200g asparagus
200g frozen peas
200g radishes, finely sliced
handful of fresh mint, chopped
handful of raisins (optional)
50g hazelnuts, toasted (see page 35) and roughly chopped
salt and pepper

FOR THE DRESSING
2 tablespoons apple cider vinegar
2 tablespoons olive oil
1 tablespoon maple syrup

Preheat the oven to 240°C (fan 220°C).

Place the carrots in a large baking tray, mixing them with the spices, a drizzle of olive oil and some salt and pepper. Roast for 10–15 minutes. Once cooked, remove and leave to cool – they should be slightly tender, but still have a good bite to them to keep the salad crunchy.

While the carrots are in the oven, remove the woody part of the asparagus and slice each one lengthways. Blanch the asparagus and peas in salted boiling water for 1 minute before refreshing in ice-cold water (you want them to have a nice crunch, and this stops them from overcooking). Drain and put both to one side.

Stir the dressing ingredients together, adding salt and pepper to taste, and once everything has cooked and cooled, place all the salad ingredients except the hazelnuts in a serving dish. Pour over the dressing and mix well, topping with the toasted hazelnuts at the end.

SIMPLE PESTO SALAD

This is another easy salad to add to your weekly dinners. We make it with aubergines, courgettes and peppers, but you could throw in any veg, so it's a nice way to use any leftovers and keep it seasonal. I like to make double quantities of the pesto, which I keep in the fridge and stir into veggie pasta, mix into salad dressings and dollop on top of rice or quinoa bowls. If you have leftovers of the salad, they're also great in a sourdough sandwich!

SERVES 4 AS A SIDE

olive oil
2 large aubergines, cut into ribbons about 1cm thick
3 courgettes, cut into ribbons about 5mm thick
2 red, orange or yellow peppers, cut into strips
pinch of sea salt
handful of almonds, toasted (see page 35) and roughly chopped
handful of fresh basil leaves, roughly chopped

FOR THE ALMOND PESTO
50ml olive oil
50g almonds, toasted (see page 35)
2 garlic cloves, roasted (see page 35)
15g basil
squeeze of lemon juice
pinch of sea salt

Preheat the oven to 200°C (fan 180°C).

Place a griddle pan over a medium heat and add a drizzle of olive oil. Once warm, add the aubergines, courgettes and peppers and grill for 5 minutes on each side until cooked through – you will need to do this in a couple of batches. Once cooked through, remove from the heat and sprinkle with the sea salt.

While the vegetables are cooking, make the pesto by placing all of the ingredients in a food processor (or a blender) with a splash of water and pulsing until smooth.

When the vegetables have cooled, mix with the pesto, making sure everything gets coated. Sprinkle with the toasted almonds and some fresh basil leaves.

TIPS

If you are making this ahead of time, don't mix the vegetables and pesto until you're ready to serve – if they're left for a long period of time, the dressing will cause the vegetables to leak water. You can also make this salad with raw vegetables instead of the aubergine, which is nice in the summer. If you're doing this just skip the roasting part of the method above.

If you have time, you can add salt to the courgettes to remove excess water. About an hour before you want to serve the salad, add a pinch of salt to the courgette ribbons and when water appears on their surface, wipe dry and repeat until you're ready to cook.

SQUASH AND CORN SALAD WITH SPICY JALAPEÑOS AND COCONUT CHIPS

The mix of tender roasted squash, sweet charred corn and coconut chips with pickled jalapeño peppers and an apple cider dressing is fantastic. There's such a great contrast between textures and flavours, sweetness and tangy sharpness. We serve this with a creamy tahini butter, lettuce salad and wild rice, and I've found it's a great summer side at a picnic or barbecue too.

**SERVES 2
AS A MAIN DISH,
4 AS A SIDE**

1 butternut squash, peeled,
    deseeded and cut into
    2.5cm cubes
olive oil
1 × 200g tin of sweetcorn,
    drained
50g pickled jalapeños, sliced
    (you can buy these in a jar)
handful of toasted coconut chips
    (about 20g)
handful of pumpkin seeds
    (about 20g)
salt and pepper

FOR THE DRESSING
1 tablespoon olive oil
1 teaspoon apple cider vinegar

Preheat the oven to 220°C (fan 200°C).

Place the squash in a large baking tray and mix with a drizzle of olive oil and some salt and pepper. Roast for 20–25 minutes.

Meanwhile, put the sweetcorn into a bowl, drizzle with olive oil, and mix with salt and pepper, then add it to the tray of squash for the last 8–10 minutes of the cooking time. Once the squash is tender and the corn slightly charred, remove the tray from the oven and leave to cool.

While the veg cools, mix the dressing ingredients, adding salt to taste. Once the vegetables are cool, place the squash and corn in a serving dish. Drizzle with the dressing, then top with the jalapeños, coconut chips, pumpkin seeds and a sprinkling of salt.

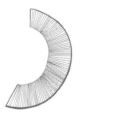

RAINBOW SALAD

This rainbow salad is a great way to up your veggie intake. It's filled with edamame, corn, rainbow chard, spring onions and avocado, which are tossed with quinoa and a maple and apple cider dressing. It's simple and delicious. I love it with the Classic hummus on page 136, which makes each bite extra creamy.

SERVES 4 AS A SIDE

250g quinoa, rinsed
100g frozen edamame beans
125g kale
1 × 200g tin of sweetcorn, drained
olive oil
35g rainbow chard, roughly
    chopped including the stem(s)
2 spring onions, roughly chopped
1 avocado, peeled, stoned and cut
    into cubes (optional)
handful of pomegranate seeds
    (optional)
salt and pepper

FOR THE DRESSING
2 tablespoons apple cider vinegar
1 tablespoon olive oil
1 tablespoon maple syrup

Preheat the oven to 240°C (fan 220°C).

Start by cooking the quinoa. Place it in a pan with 500ml water, bring to the boil, then let it simmer for about 12–15 minutes, adding the edamame for the last minute or two. Drain and leave to cool.

While they cook, strip the kale off its stalks and tear it into pieces (discard the stalks). Then place the kale and corn in a baking tray (keeping them separate if possible) with a drizzle of olive oil and some salt and pepper and roast in the oven for 5–10 minutes, until the corn starts to char and the kale turns a little crispy.

While the vegetables are cooking, stir the dressing ingredients together.

Once everything is ready, place the sweetcorn, quinoa, edamame beans, rainbow chard and dressing in a large bowl and mix well. Finally, stir through the kale and spring onions and add the chunks of avocado and pomegranate seeds, if using, just before serving.

TIP
This is a great salad to make if you are trying to avoid food waste. If you have any leftover vegetables you can throw them in. We've even used roasted chunks of broccoli stem in the past, which were delicious, as were chunks of beetroot.

SPICED PEANUT SWEET POTATOES

I think this is my favourite recipe in the book; I'm completely addicted to it. The sweet potatoes are roasted with ginger, cinnamon and cumin until they're perfectly tender, then they're tossed with sesame seeds, dates, parsley and a smooth peanut butter dressing while still warm. They're heaven! I eat these on their own, because they're just so good, but they are a great side too. At the deli we sometimes serve this with chopped radicchio, which is a delicious addition and adds some more colour to the dish.

SERVES 4 AS A SIDE

2 large sweet potatoes, peeled
    and cut into small cubes
2 tablespoons olive oil
2 teaspoons ground ginger
2 teaspoons ground cinnamon
2 teaspoons ground cumin
handful of parsley, chopped
45g dates, pitted and chopped
1 heaped tablespoon black sesame
    seeds (normal sesame seeds
    also work – you'll just need
    to toast them)
salt and pepper

FOR THE DRESSING
2 tablespoons date syrup
    or maple syrup
2 tablespoons sesame oil
2 tablespoons smooth
    peanut butter
juice of ½ lemon

TO SERVE
handful of peanuts, toasted
    (see page 35) and chopped
    (optional)

Preheat the oven to 240°C (fan 220°C).

Place the sweet potatoes in a large baking tray and drizzle with the olive oil, add the spices and some salt and pepper and mix well, ensuring everything gets coated. Bake in the oven for 45–50 minutes, until they're really soft.

While the sweet potatoes are cooking, make the dressing, whisking everything with some salt until smooth.

Next, place the parsley and dates in a large bowl with the sesame seeds. Once the sweet potatoes are cooked, add them to the bowl with the dressing and mix everything together. Sprinkle with toasted peanuts, if using, serve and enjoy.

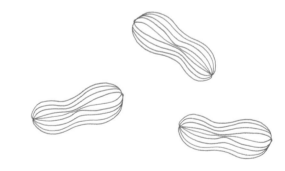

TIP
This dish is most delicious served hot straight out the oven but it also works well at room temperature.

OLIVE AND SUN-DRIED TOMATO QUINOA

This is my go-to quinoa recipe and something I make all the time. The olives, parsley and sun-dried tomatoes with the sweet sultanas and toasted almonds gives it so much flavour. I find this goes well with so many different dishes. Try it with our Sweet potato cakes, Baked butter bean and cauliflower falafel or Mushroom and chestnut sliders (see pages 126, 122 and 131), or some simple roasted veg.

SERVES 2
AS A MAIN DISH,
4 AS A SIDE

250g quinoa, rinsed
65g black olives, pitted
135g sun-dried tomatoes in oil (drained weight), finely chopped
25g parsley, chopped
35g sultanas or raisins, soaked in boiling water for 10 minutes, then drained
40g almonds, toasted (see page 35) and roughly chopped
salt and pepper

FOR THE DRESSING
juice of 1 lemon
1 tablespoon balsamic vinegar
3 tablespoons olive oil from the sun-dried tomato jar

Preheat the oven to 200°C (fan 180°C).

Start by cooking the quinoa. Place it in a pan with 500ml water, bring to the boil then let it simmer for 12–15 minutes. Drain and leave to cool.

Meanwhile, stir the dressing ingredients together with some salt and pepper.

Next, place the olives, sun-dried tomatoes and parsley in a mixing bowl along with the sultanas and most of the almonds. Give it all a good mix.

Once the quinoa has cooled, add it to the bowl, along with the dressing and mix well. Sprinkle the remaining almonds over the top before serving.

SPICED NEW POTATOES WITH MINTY YOGHURT DRESSING

This is a nice way to spice up new potatoes. They're tossed with cayenne pepper, oregano, paprika and thyme and then baked until golden, at which point we stir watercress through for a pop of colour and dollop a minty yoghurt dressing over the top. You can also skip the dressing and watercress and serve this hot out the oven just with the spice mix.

SERVES 4 AS A SIDE

500g new potatoes, halved
olive oil
1 teaspoon cayenne pepper
1 teaspoon paprika
1 teaspoon dried oregano
1 teaspoon dried thyme
50g watercress, rinsed
salt

FOR THE DRESSING
100g plain yoghurt (we use
    a pure coconut yoghurt)
1 tablespoon lemon juice
handful of mint,
    roughly chopped
1 tablespoon olive oil

Preheat the oven to 245°C (fan 225°C).

Mix the potatoes with a good drizzle of olive oil, some salt and all the spices and dried herbs. Cook for 35–40 minutes, until soft and golden. Once cooked, remove from the oven.

Make the dressing by stirring everything together with some salt, to taste.

Mix the watercress through the potatoes and spoon dollops of the dressing on to the potatoes before serving.

SPICY MISO AUBERGINE AND BROCCOLI SALAD

This salad was a real hit in the deli, and it's one of my go-tos as well. We used to serve it cool, but have recently discovered a new love of serving it warm, straight out the oven and couldn't recommend that more. The dressing is partly what makes this so good and I use it a lot in other dishes – the ginger, miso, sesame and lime mix is a real winner.

**SERVES 2
AS A MAIN DISH,
4 AS A SIDE**

2 medium aubergines, chopped
    into bite-sized chunks
1 large head of broccoli, chopped
    into florets
pinch of chilli flakes
handful of coriander, chopped
handful of sesame seeds
salt and pepper

FOR THE MISO DRESSING
4 tablespoons miso paste
juice of 1 lime
1 tablespoon rice vinegar
3 tablespoons sesame oil
1 thumb-sized piece of ginger,
    peeled and grated

Preheat the oven to 240°C (fan 220°C).

For the dressing, blitz the miso, lime juice, vinegar, sesame oil, ginger and some salt and pepper in a blender until smooth. If you don't have a blender, dissolve the miso paste in a tablespoon of boiling water then stir through the other dressing ingredients.

In a large baking tray, mix the aubergine with the dressing and roast for 30–35 minutes. At this point, remove the tray from the oven and switch the oven over to the grill setting. Mix the broccoli florets with the aubergine, then place the tray back in the oven for another 10 minutes until the broccoli is lightly charred on top and the aubergine is soft and golden.

Once cooked, remove from the oven, place in a serving bowl and sprinkle with the chilli flakes, coriander and sesame seeds before serving.

TURMERIC SPICED CAULIFLOWER, LENTIL AND TAHINI SALAD

We served this salad on the day we opened the deli and have loved it ever since. The mix of creamy tahini with turmeric roasted cauliflower, lentils, fresh parsley and sultanas is a real crowd-pleaser. It's great with our Baked sweet potato falafel and some Classic hummus (see pages 118 and 136).

**SERVES 2
AS A MAIN DISH,
4 AS A SIDE**

250g dried green lentils
60g sultanas
1 large cauliflower (or two small cauliflowers), cut into small florets
2 tablespoons olive oil
2 teaspoons ground turmeric
1 teaspoon ground cumin
1 teaspoon chilli flakes
handful of parsley, roughly chopped
handful of spinach (optional)
salt

FOR THE DRESSING
1 tablespoon lemon juice
2 tablespoons olive oil
2 garlic cloves, roasted (see page 35)
2 heaped tablespoons tahini

Preheat the oven to 245°C (fan 225°C).

Place the lentils in a pan filled with water and cook over a medium heat for 20 minutes until soft. Once cooked, drain and rinse with cold water to stop them from cooking any further.

Meanwhile, put the sultanas into a bowl of warm water and soak for 5–10 minutes. Once soaked, drain and leave to one side – this softens them and makes them juicy.

While the lentils are cooking, place the cauliflower florets in a large baking tray and mix with the olive oil, turmeric, cumin, chili flakes and some salt, ensuring the florets are evenly coated. Roast for 10–15 minutes. Once cooked, remove and leave to one side while you whisk the dressing ingredients in a small bowl.

Once everything has cooked, mix all of the salad ingredients in a serving bowl and stir through the dressing.

TIP
Although it's optional, adding the spinach gives a great pop of colour, which is lovely if you're serving this to friends and family. You can also try sprinkling it with pomegranate seeds or chopped herbs.

ZESTY PEA, QUINOA AND RADISH SALAD

This is a perfect summer salad: fresh, light and vibrant. The radishes, peas and mint add great pops of colour, while the spring onions, lemon and cider vinegar give it a zesty flavour. At the deli we served this with our Classic hummus (see page 136) and some cinnamon-roasted sweet potatoes, although it's great with our Pea, broad bean and basil dip (see page 139) too.

**SERVES 2
AS A MAIN DISH,
4 AS A SIDE**

250g quinoa (we like using
 a mix of the three colours
 in ours, but that's optional)
250g frozen peas
10 radishes, thinly sliced
25g mint, roughly chopped
6 spring onions, thinly sliced
salt and pepper

FOR THE DRESSING
2 tablespoons olive oil
2 tablespoons apple cider vinegar
juice of 1 lemon

Start by cooking the quinoa. Place in a pan with 500ml water, bring to the boil then let it simmer for about 12–15 minutes. Drain and leave to cool.

While the quinoa is cooking, blanch the peas in boiling water for 1 minute before refreshing in ice-cold water to stop them from cooking further. Drain and leave to one side.

Mix the dressing ingredients with some salt and pepper, and once the quinoa is cool, place all the ingredients in a bowl, stirring through the dressing.

HARISSA-ROASTED AUBERGINES

I love harissa; it's a spicy chilli paste and adds great flavour to anything that can stand up to its heat. You can easily buy the paste, but if you'd like to make your own we use the recipe below. The aubergines are tossed in a dressing of the harissa, pomegranate molasses, cayenne pepper and maple then roasted until they're soft and tender. They're delicious served warm, but they're also great cooled and served as a salad.

SERVES 4
AS A MAIN DISH,
8 AS A SIDE

4 tablespoons harissa paste
    (shop-bought or see below)
2 tablespoons olive oil
2 tablespoons pomegranate
    molasses
2 tablespoons maple syrup
½ teaspoon cayenne pepper
    (optional)
4 medium aubergines, cut into
    bite-sized chunks
salt and pepper

FOR THE HARISSA PASTE
280g roasted peppers from a jar,
    drained, plus 3 tablespoons
    of its oil
1 red chilli, sliced
3 garlic cloves, roasted (see
    page 35)
3 tablespoons smoked paprika
3 tablespoons tomato purée
1 teaspoon ground cumin
1 teaspoon fennel seeds
1 teaspoon ground coriander

TO SERVE (OPTIONAL)
a sprinkle of sesame seeds,
    toasted in a dry pan

Preheat the oven to 240°C (fan 220°C).

If you're making your own harissa paste, simply place all the ingredients into a food processor with some salt and pepper and blitz until smooth. Store in an airtight jar in the fridge for about a week.

Mix 4 tablespoons of the harissa paste with the olive oil, pomegranate molasses, maple syrup, cayenne pepper, if using, and some salt in a bowl.

Place the aubergine in a large baking tray. Pour the dressing in and give everything a really good mix, making sure all of the aubergine pieces are nicely coated in the dressing. Roast for 40–45 minutes, until soft and delicious. Sprinkle with a handful of sesame seeds.

TIP
Use your leftover harissa in dressings, on top of roast veg, spread into a sourdough sandwich or dolloped on to quinoa bowls. It's a lovely way to add more flavour to something simple. If you can't find harissa paste and don't want to make it, then try something like a roasted red pepper paste.

WHOLE BAKED CAULIFLOWER

This whole cauliflower is a real beauty and a great centrepiece for any table. We bake it with a turmeric, smoked paprika, cumin and coriander crust, which turns it a wonderful colour and adds such great flavour. I serve it alongside warm Harissa-roasted aubergines, Smoky aubergine dip and Black rice salad (pages 108, 140 and 228).

SERVES 4 AS A SIDE

4 tablespoons olive oil
1 large cauliflower
2 tablespoons smoked paprika
1 tablespoon ground turmeric
1 teaspoon ground cumin
1 teaspoon ground coriander
salt

Preheat the oven to 200°C (fan 180°C).

Drizzle the olive oil over the cauliflower and sprinkle it with salt. Mix together the paprika, turmeric, cumin and coriander, and, using your hands, rub the spice mix on to the cauliflower to form a crust.

Place in the oven for 1–1¼ hours, or until cooked through. The cooking time really depends on the size of your cauliflower, so keep an eye on it and give it a little more time in the oven if needed.

Once it's tender all the way through, remove and serve warm.

TIP
Try mixing up the spices here – it's nice with a little chilli powder or cayenne pepper, or intensify the flavours by adding a spoonful of harissa paste from the Harissa-roasted aubergines (see page 108) to the spice mix.

FALAFEL, BURGERS AND DIPS

The Deliciously Ella Diary
— *part 3*

By mid-December 2016, we had two delis open, lots of delicious new recipes for our customers and our range of energy balls had been successfully launched. We were so excited with how the business was going and we couldn't believe it when we walked into a shop and saw our products for sale or watched a customer enjoy one of our new dishes. But we felt like there was still so much more to do. Matt and I had planned a quiet Christmas with our families to regroup, then, in the New Year, wanted to focus on innovation for our product business and expanding our team for the next stage of growth. However, these plans were dependent on us raising investment. It was something we had been working on for the previous six months and was desperately needed, as although our business was growing, we had a huge number of large payments due at the end of December and had agreed with the investor that he'd fund this shortfall before he went away for Christmas. However, on the day before signing our deal, the terms were suddenly changed and we were put in a near-impossible situation: sign a terrible deal or run out of money by the 1st January and consequently go bust. One of the biggest problems was the timing; everything was about to shut for Christmas, so the bank couldn't look into loans or an extension of our overdraft until the New Year, but we had no way to cover the huge payments due before January.

Suffice it to say, it was a really stressful stage and one of the scariest moments we've had to date. We had employed people with families, who had come to us from secure jobs, and had new starters confirmed, but there was seemingly no way to keep the business afloat without doing something we knew wouldn't serve us in the long run. After an agonising few days, we decided to walk away from the deal and instead accept a short-term loan from our finance director, our family and a friend, which we secured against our flat. Knowing that we now owed our parents and other people we cared for so much money was terrifying. At this point, everything we had – both emotionally and materially – was invested in Deliciously Ella.

On the outside, things, I'm sure, looked pretty great, especially as our energy balls were in more than 3,000 stores just six months after launch. Internally though, it felt as though we were just fighting to survive, and we were on a pretty intense mission to get cash into the business. We were still based in our tiny, 450 square-foot office on Bloomsbury Street with all the honking and beeping that comes from a busy one-way road on which there's nowhere to stop. When I'd taken on the lease in 2015, just before meeting Matt, I

> OUR TEAM FOUND THEMSELVES IN A SPACE WHERE THERE WAS A KITCHEN IN THE MIDDLE OF THE ROOM, BLENDERS WOULD BE WHIZZING WHILE THEY MADE IMPORTANT CALLS, AND AUSTIN WOULD JUMP ON TO THEIR CHAIR TO STEAL IT!

had assumed that we'd never be more than five people or so, but at this point we had between 14 and 17 people in there on any day. Our team had left their sensible professional environments and found themselves in a space where no one had a permanent desk, there was a kitchen in the middle of the room, blenders would be whizzing while they made important calls, I would stand on their desk to get a good Instagram photo and

every time they stood up our dog Austin would jump on to their unoccupied chair and steal it for himself! Due to the lack of space, we used the little hotel opposite us for our meetings and the staircase for conference calls. It was mad, but there was a real buzz in there every day and it definitely helped to bring us all together. Matt kept telling us that he was going to build a mezzanine level to fit some more bodies in and we all laughed, but I really don't think he was joking – if he could have, he would have!

Our office lease was due to run out at the end of May though, so that spurred us on with the search for new investors. The whole process felt a little bit like speed dating; we met so many people and it was a question of whether there was a spark, a sense of mutual respect, excitement and a comfortable acceptance of the fact that we would be tied up together for years. We pitched to a lot of people, but we knew as soon as we'd met the right group. We both had the same gut instinct, and that sense

of intuition is something we try and listen to a lot in our business. We had to do a Dragons' Den style pitch to them, and I was the only woman in a room of about 40 men, all of whom were phenomenally successful. I couldn't help but feel a little intimidated, but once I'd got past my own fear, things went really well and we started progressing with a deal soon afterwards.

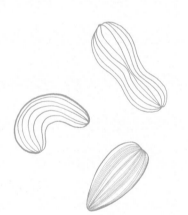

We'd been so desperate for cash that I hadn't completely taken stock of what a huge thing it was for me to give some of Deliciously Ella to what felt like total strangers. Handing over part of the business I had created was a crazy feeling but I knew it was right. From this moment, what we were doing was no longer about me, it was about our team members; our new investors, who had trusted us with their money; and, most importantly, the Deliciously Ella community, whom I knew we could do more for with additional funds. As terrifying as it was, the second the papers were signed there was a real sense of relief. We were able to pay back the money we'd recently borrowed, the business had some money in it, and despite still having the loan against our flat, we were stable for the first time, and really excited to see what would happen next. Matt and I lay in bed that night, cried a bit with relief, and looked forward to waking up the next morning on more solid ground.

THERE WERE STILL INTENSE PERIODS, AND WE DID KEEP WORKING AROUND THE CLOCK, EVEN CANCELLING OUR ROMANTIC WEDDING ANNIVERSARY WEEKEND IN PARIS TO SIT IN A PORTAKABIN EATING KILOS OF GRANOLA

The first thing we did was upgrade our office. We moved into our new company home in Soho in central London in May 2017, where we've built a dream kitchen which we all love. It has a beautiful white marble work surface and gorgeous wooden shelves, which you'll see throughout the book. It's an amazing place to work, and we have plant-based team breakfasts and lunches in there every day, as well as filming and shooting all our recipes for the blog and social channels.

Around the same time, we also opened a big kitchen in Herne Hill in south London. This was the ideal spot as we could use it as a base from which to cater for the delis. We also opened our third deli there.

From this point, things continued to grow quickly: we scaled up the team, launched our next book and got to work on the second product range – our granolas and bircher muesli. There were still intense periods, and we did keep working around the clock, even cancelling our romantic wedding anniversary weekend in Paris to sit in a Portakabin eating kilos and kilos of granola to meet a supermarket deadline, but each day felt more and

more exciting. I was also really focused on making Deliciously Ella more accessible. Working as hard as we were, I was always short on time and knew that was the case for so many others – we all needed quick, simple recipes and ideas that worked within our day-to-day to-do lists, as well as using ingredients that were mostly easy to get hold of and that's what forms the basis of the recipes in this chapter.

BAKED SWEET POTATO FALAFEL

These sweet potato falafel have been on our menu since we opened and we've had lots of requests for the recipe, so I hope you enjoy making them at home. They're really simple to make and need just six kitchen cupboard ingredients. I love these with salads and lots of hummus. They're perfect for on-the-go and desk lunches too.

MAKES 10

2 medium sweet potatoes (about 300g), peeled and cut into bite-sized chunks
olive oil
1 × 400g tin of chickpeas, drained and rinsed
2 tablespoons gram flour or plain flour
2 garlic cloves, roasted (see page 35)
1 teaspoon ground cumin
1 teaspoon smoked paprika
salt and pepper

Preheat the oven to 220°C (fan 200°C).

Place the chunks of sweet potato in a baking tray with a drizzle of olive oil and some salt and pepper, then put the tray into the oven for 40–45 minutes, until the sweet potatoes are soft. At this point, take them out and leave to cool.

Once the potatoes are cool, place them in a food processor along with all the remaining ingredients and pulse until you have a smooth paste.

Scoop balls of the mixture out of the food processor using an ice-cream scoop, smooth them a little by rolling them in your hands if you like, then place them on a lined baking sheet and bake in the oven for 30 minutes. Check they're cooked through by inserting a knife into the middle of one ball – if it comes out clean they're ready, if not bake for a little longer.

TIP
These falafel are delicious served warm straight out the oven with a hot salad, such as the Roast squash, spring onion and mixed rice salad (see page 81), but they are also nice served cool.

BAKED SUN-DRIED TOMATO FALAFEL

This is my favourite falafel recipe. I love the rich flavour of the sun-dried tomatoes and the blend of chickpeas, butter beans, garlic, parsley and lemon juice. They're really quick to make and are always a real hit. I love serving them as little appetisers with hummus to dunk them in when friends come over.

MAKES 10

1 × 400g tin of butter beans, drained and rinsed
½ × 400g tin of chickpeas, drained and rinsed
90g sun-dried tomatoes in oil (drained weight), plus 2 tablespoons of oil from the jar
2 garlic cloves, roasted (see page 35)
handful of parsley, chopped
2 tablespoons tomato purée
squeeze of lemon juice
salt and pepper

Preheat the oven to 220°C (fan 200°C).

Place all the ingredients in a food processor and pulse until you have a smooth paste.

Scoop balls of the mixture out of the food processor using an ice-cream scoop, smooth them a little by rolling them in your hands if you like, then place them on a lined baking sheet and bake in the oven for 30 minutes. Check they're cooked through by inserting a knife into the middle of one ball – if it comes out clean they're ready, if not bake for a little longer.

TIP
Try making mini versions of these – about half the size of the ones in the recipe – to serve as little appetisers.

BAKED BUTTER BEAN AND CAULIFLOWER FALAFEL

Cauliflower and butter beans bring a creaminess to whatever they're used in, which is exactly what they do here – they add softness to each bite. The cumin, chilli and garlic give these falafel a fantastic flavour.

MAKES 10

½ cauliflower (about 200g), cut into small florets
1 × 400g tin butter beans, drained and rinsed
1 × 400g tin of chickpeas, drained and rinsed
2 garlic cloves, roasted (see page 35)
2 tablespoons olive oil
1 small red chilli (deseeded if you like less spice)
30g ground almonds
2 teaspoons ground cumin
1 teaspoon paprika
1 teaspoon ground coriander
1 tablespoon olive oil
salt and pepper

Preheat the oven to 220°C (fan 200°C).

Place the cauliflower in a roasting tray and roast in the oven (without oil) for 8 minutes – it should still be crunchy at this point. Remove and leave to cool.

When the cauliflower is completely cool, place it in a food processor along with all the remaining ingredients. Pulse until the mixture comes together as a smooth paste. Once combined, place in the fridge for 1–2 hours. The cauliflower makes this falafel mixture a bit thinner than our other recipes, so chilling the mixture ensures it is thick enough to hold its shape. While the mixture sets in the fridge, you can turn your oven off.

Turn your oven on again to heat to 220°C (fan 200°C).

Scoop balls of the mixture out of the food processor using an ice-cream scoop, smooth them a little by rolling them in your hands if you like, then place them on a lined baking sheet and bake in the oven for 30 minutes. Check they're cooked through by inserting a knife into the middle of one ball – if it comes out clean they're ready, if not bake for a little longer.

TIP
If you want to add extra flavour, add a handful of chopped parsley or some more spices to the falafel – a sprinkling of paprika or cayenne pepper is delicious.

HERBED LENTIL BALLS WITH TOMATO RELISH AND GARLIC CREAM

I know these may sound a little strange, but they taste amazing – especially sitting in a bed of tomato relish and dressed with garlic cream. They're full of flavour thanks to the thyme, rosemary, parsley, garlic and onion. I love them served simply with some brown rice and salad.

MAKES 10

150g dried green lentils
1 large onion, sliced
2 garlic cloves, sliced
2 tablespoons buckwheat flour
2 tablespoons olive oil
handful of parsley, roughly chopped
1 teaspoon dried thyme
1 teaspoon dried rosemary
salt and pepper

FOR THE TOMATO RELISH
6 tablespoons tomato purée
3 garlic cloves, peeled
2 teaspoons balsamic vinegar
1 teaspoon maple syrup
100ml water
handful of parsley
pinch of ground cumin
pinch of chilli powder
pinch of smoked paprika

FOR THE GARLIC CREAM
100g cashews, soaked for at least 3 hours then drained
10 tablespoons almond milk
3 garlic cloves, roasted (see page 35)
splash of lemon juice

Preheat the oven to 200°C (fan 180°C).

Start by placing the lentils in a pan of boiling water. Cook for 20–25 minutes until tender but still with a slight bite. Once cooked, drain and leave to cool to room temperature.

While the lentils are cooking, place the onion and garlic in a pan over a medium heat with a drizzle of olive oil and some salt and cook for 5–10 minutes, until soft. Then leave to cool to room temperature.

Place all of the ingredients in a food processor and pulse until they form a thick paste. Scoop balls of the mixture out of the food processor using an ice-cream scoop, smooth them a little by rolling them in your hands if you like, then place them on a baking tray and bake in the oven for 35–40 minutes. Check the lentil balls are cooked through by inserting a knife into the middle of one ball – if it comes out clean they're ready, if not bake for a little longer.

While the balls are in the oven, prepare the tomato relish and garlic cream. Simply place all of the ingredients for the relish in a food processor and some salt and pulse until smooth. Then do the same for the garlic cream, adding salt and pepper to taste. Serve the lentil balls piled high with the relish and garlic cream.

TIP
These are delicious served warm straight out the oven – if you're doing that then gently warm the tomato relish too.

SWEET POTATO CAKES

These little sweet potato cakes are a great addition to any meal. I love them as part of a simple lunch bowl with brown rice and green veg, or served in a little stack with our Smoky baked beans (see page 65) and sliced avocado for brunch. Make extra as they're easy to pop into a container for an on-the-go meal, plus you can freeze any extra cakes too – just fry them, leave them to cool, then freeze.

MAKES 14

300g sweet potato (about
    2–3 sweet potatoes)
1 red onion
1 garlic clove
olive oil
1 teaspoon ground ginger
1 tablespoon arrowroot
2 spring onions, finely sliced
1 heaped tablespoon
    coconut oil, melted,
    plus extra for frying
salt and pepper

Preheat the oven to 220°C (fan 200°C).

Peel and grate the sweet potato, place in a baking tray covered with foil and cook in the oven for 20–25 minutes until soft. The foil will help to lock in the moisture and ensure the sweet potatoes cook through evenly.

While the sweet potatoes are cooking, finely slice the onion and garlic. Place them in a pan over a medium heat, drizzle with olive oil and cook for 5–10 minutes, until soft.

Once the sweet potatoes are cooked, mix them with the onion, garlic, ginger, arrowroot, spring onions, the melted coconut oil and some salt and pepper.

Place a frying pan over a medium heat with a little more coconut oil. Using a tablespoon, spoon out balls of the mixture and press down into little patties, about 5cm across. Cook in the pan for 3–4 minutes on each side, until golden.

MYLKS

…0ml £6.95

…Juice

…lk

…lk

DRINKS

Made with your choice of almond,
coconut or oat mylk

HOT

Espresso
Americano
Latte
Mocha   £2.50
Matcha Latte   £2.75
Turmeric Latte   £3.25
Hot Chocolate   £3.50
Organic Tea   £3.50
    £3.50
    £2.50

ICED

Iced Coffee   £3.50
Iced Matcha   £3.50

MUSHROOM AND CHESTNUT SLIDERS

These little mushroom and chestnut sliders are so delicious and have lovely hints of cumin, garlic and thyme. The flavour is rich, but the texture is soft and light. I love them served with salad bowls or in little sourdough buns with lots of hot sauce, slices of creamy avocado and some crispy lettuce. If you like a bit of sauce, the Tomato relish on page 125 is perfect with these.

MAKES 20 SMALL SLIDERS

600g chestnut mushrooms, roughly chopped
2 garlic cloves, chopped
4 teaspoons dried thyme
1 teaspoon ground cumin
olive oil
360g cooked chestnuts
1 heaped tablespoon plain flour (we use a gluten-free one)
2 teaspoons arrowroot
salt and pepper

Preheat the oven to 220°C (fan 200°C).

In a bowl toss the mushrooms with the garlic, thyme, cumin, a drizzle of olive oil and some salt and pepper. Place the mixture in a baking tray and roast for 10–15 minutes until the mushrooms are golden, then remove and leave to cool.

Once cool, place the mushrooms in a food processor with all of the other ingredients and pulse until smooth. Scoop out one heaped tablespoon of the mixture at a time and form small patties, about 5cm across, using your hands.

Place a frying pan with a drizzle of olive oil over a medium heat and cook the sliders for 3–4 minutes on each side, until firm and cooked through.

QUINOA AND BLACK BEAN BURGERS

We made these burgers for an Action Against Hunger burger-themed supper club and they were such a hit that we knew we needed to share them with you. They're so easy to make and the mix of quinoa, black beans, mushrooms and chilli is delicious.

MAKES 6 LARGE BURGERS

1 red onion, finely chopped
2 garlic cloves, roasted
   (see page 35)
olive oil
½ teaspoon cayenne pepper
1 teaspoon smoked paprika
1 teaspoon chilli powder
150g chestnut mushrooms
125g quinoa
250ml boiling water
1 × 400g tin of black beans,
   drained and rinsed
1 heaped tablespoon plain flour
   (we use a gluten-free one)
1 teaspoon arrowroot
pinch of sea salt annd pepper

Preheat the oven to 220°C (fan 200°C).

Place the onion and garlic in a frying pan over a medium heat with a drizzle of olive oil and cook for 5–10 minutes, until soft. Add the spices and cook for another minute before removing from the heat and leaving to cool.

Place the mushrooms in a baking tray with a tablespoon of olive oil and some salt and pepper and roast for 10–15 minutes until golden. Remove and leave to cool.

While the mushrooms cook, prepare the quinoa by placing it in a pan over a medium heat and covering with the boiling water. Bring back to the boil and simmer for 10–15 minutes. Once cooked, remove and leave to cool.

Once the mushrooms and quinoa have cooled, place all the ingredients in a food processor – make sure you discard any excess liquid from the mushroom pan before adding them to the processor, as this can make the mix too watery. Pulse until smooth then place the mixture in the fridge to cool for 30 minutes.

Once cool, use a large spoon to scoop out patties and flatten them into round shapes, about 8cm across. If needed, place the patties in the fridge for another 30 minutes to firm up.

Once the patties are firm enough to hold together when flipped; place a frying pan over a medium heat, drizzle with olive oil and cook the burgers for 5 minutes on each side.

TIP
These freeze well, so put any patties you don't need straight away in the freezer for another day or keep in the fridge for a few days and have them cold as part of an on-the-go or desk lunch.

CREAMY AVOCADO DIP

This brightly-coloured dip feels like a mix between guacamole, hummus and pesto – three of my favourite things! The basil adds great flavour, while the chickpeas thicken it up and the avocado makes it so creamy. We add garlic and lemon juice to enhance the flavour.

MAKES 1 BOWL (ENOUGH TO SERVE ABOUT 4)

2 ripe medium avocados, peeled, stoned and roughly chopped
1 × 400g tin of chickpeas, drained and rinsed
juice of ½ lemon
2 tablespoons olive oil
2 garlic cloves, roasted (see page 35)
25g basil
salt and pepper

Simply place all of the ingredients in a food processor and pulse until smooth.

TIP
This is best served fresh to keep the colour. It's delicious served with a mix of toasted rye bread and crunchy veggies or layered into a grain bowl.

HUMMUS

EACH RECIPE
MAKES 1 BOWL
(ENOUGH TO
SERVE ABOUT 4)

These are simple recipes, but nice ones to have up your sleeve, as they're quick and easy to make and hummus works well with just about everything. I make big batches of these every week so that I always have some in the fridge. I slather hummus on toast, dollop it on to salads and grain bowls, dip corn chips into it and even eat it with a spoon straight out the bowl. Classic hummus is a go-to for most of us, the roasted squash one is so incredibly creamy and the piquillo pepper one has a sweet, roasted red pepper flavour.

CLASSIC

2 × 400g tins of chickpeas,
    plus the water from 1 tin
3 teaspoons ground cumin
juice of 1 lemon
115ml olive oil
2 garlic cloves, roasted
    (see page 35)
3 tablespoons tahini
salt

PIQUILLO PEPPER
AND WALNUT

1 × 400g tin of chickpeas, plus
    3 tablespoons of water from
    the tin
150g piquillo peppers
2 tablespoons olive oil
2 garlic cloves, roasted (see page 35)
Juice of 1 lemon
3 tablespoons tahini
2 tablespoons maple syrup
50g walnuts, toasted (see page 35)
salt

Drain and rinse the chickpeas and place them in a food processor with all of the other ingredients. Whizz until smooth and creamy.

TIP

Piquillo peppers are a mild variety of chilli. You should be able to find them in the supermarket in a jar quite easily but, if you can't, just use any kind of jarred pepper.

ROASTED
BUTTERNUT
SQUASH

700g butternut squash, peeled,
    deseeded and cubed
8 tablespoons olive oil, plus an
    extra drizzle for the squash
1 × 400g tin of chickpeas,
    drained and rinsed
2 garlic cloves, roasted
    (see page 35)
juice of ½ lemon
2 tablespoons tahini
1 teaspoon dried cumin
salt and pepper

Preheat the oven to 220°C (fan 200°C).

Place the chunks of squash in a baking tray with a drizzle of olive oil and some salt and pepper. Roast in the oven for 45–50 minutes, until tender. Once cooked, remove and leave to cool.

Once the squash is cool, place it in a food processor with all the remaining ingredients and whizz until smooth and creamy.

TIP

When serving these to friends, I like topping them with some garnishes to make them look even more beautiful. I add smoked paprika, olive oil and a sprinkling of roasted chickpeas to the classic; olive oil, chilli flakes and chopped walnuts to the piquillo pepper one; and some chopped parsley and olive oil to the butternut squash recipe.

PEA, BROAD BEAN AND BASIL DIP

If you're looking for a change from hummus, this is a great option, as it uses broad beans instead of chickpeas and has a different flavour but the same kind of texture. It works well served with crunchy crudités or as a side in a big salad spread – I love the taste of the peas and avocado together. It is also a great way to sneak lots of extra veggies into a meal and add an extra dose of green to your life.

MAKES 1 BOWL (ENOUGH TO SERVE ABOUT 4)

1 large shallot, peeled and chopped
2 garlic cloves, chopped
olive oil
1 × 300g tin of broad beans, drained and rinsed
130g fresh peas (podded weight) or use frozen
1 avocado, peeled, stoned and roughly chopped
handful of fresh basil, chopped
2 tablespoons lemon juice
salt

Place the shallot and garlic in a frying pan over a medium heat with a drizzle of olive oil and cook for 5–10 minutes, until soft, then leave to one side to cool.

Meanwhile, blanch the broad beans and peas in boiling water for 2–3 minutes, before cooling in ice-cold water. Once cool, drain and leave to one side.

Once cool, place all of the ingredients in a food processor and pulse until smooth, adding a little salt to your taste.

TIP
This dip tastes delicious garnished with a drizzle of olive oil and a handful of toasted sunflower seeds.

SMOKY AUBERGINE DIP

I'm pretty obsessed with this dip and make it as often as I can. The mix of roasted aubergines with tahini, sesame oil, peanut butter, garlic and lemon is just incredible. It's bursting with flavour, and the smooth, creamy texture is wonderful too. I love adding this to salads, as well as serving it as a dip before dinner when I have friends round.

**MAKES 1 BOWL
(ENOUGH TO
SERVE ABOUT 4)**

3 medium aubergines
olive oil
4 garlic cloves
juice of ½ lemon
1 tablespoon tahini
1 tablespoon smooth
    peanut butter
1 tablespoon sesame oil
1 teaspoon smoked paprika
salt and pepper

Preheat the oven to 220°C (fan 200°C).

Peel the aubergines and halve them lengthways. Place in a baking tray, drizzle with olive oil and add some salt and pepper. Roast for 40–45 minutes, until golden, adding the garlic for the last 5–10 minutes. Once cooked, remove and leave to cool.

Once the aubergine is cool, scrape the flesh into a food processor, along with the rest of the ingredients and pulse until smooth.

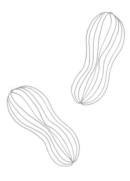

TIP
This dip is delicious served with a drizzle of olive oil and sprinkled with a handful of pomegranate seeds.

WARMING SOUPS, STEWS, CURRIES AND MORE

The Deliciously Ella Diary
— *part 4*

Momentum in the business started building from spring 2017, fuelled by lots of warming bowls of our Five-bean chilli with corn bread and our all-time favourite Green Thai curry (see pages 162–5 and 174). It felt as though we were finding our rhythm and that the sky was the limit, so we put lots of plans in motion and thought we'd spend the summer getting them going. Between June and September, we planned to refurbish the delis, change the format of their entire menu, launch two granolas and a bircher muesli into supermarkets, get ready to introduce our existing ranges and a new oat bar range (which we also had to create, source and produce) into Tesco, start work on this book and begin photographing it, take the deli to Wilderness Festival and Manchester Food Festival, revamp the app and a whole host of other projects. It was an ambitious project plan as it was, and then, out of absolutely nowhere, we were hit with our biggest challenge yet.

I wrote this chapter with Matt's blessing, as it's something that impacted on him and on us so profoundly that we both felt it was important to share it. When I started Deliciously Ella, I made a decision to open up about the mental and physical challenges I'd been through with my illness. As we grew, I continued to share my thoughts and feelings, however, I respected the privacy of my family and never shared anything that involved anyone else. This was especially relevant to my parents' separation and divorce, which got complicated and very emotionally charged at moments, and unfolded alongside everything we've talked about so far in the book. At moments, posting upbeat pictures of porridge and quinoa bowls felt at odds with the authentic and open nature of Deliciously Ella when I was sitting on the sofa crying, but equally my family mean more to me than anything, and it was right to keep those details private for their sake. The next family challenge, however, was something that we wanted to talk about, as we hope it resonates with anyone going through something similar.

I was working in New York for a week at the end of May getting everything wrapped up for the launch of the US edition of *Deliciously Ella with Friends* later that year, and Matt, after not really taking any time off in two years, had just arrived to play golf with three friends in Scotland for a few days. Just as Matt walked into his hotel, he got a call from the police telling him that his mum had been brought into the police station and was having a seizure. Matt, his mum, and the rest of their family are as close as you could possibly imagine. In fact, I've never seen anything like it. It's been incredibly inspiring to be a part of, and they couldn't have welcomed me into it more warmly. When Matt called me, I had never heard despair like it in someone's voice. His mum was now en route to hospital but they weren't sure if she was going to make it through the night. We both scrambled back to London immediately, to learn, after two days of tests, that Matt's mum, Tessa, had brain cancer. The following week, after emergency surgery, we found out that it was grade four and incredibly aggressive. Matt was broken and our world was immediately put on hold. For the first time in two years we turned our phones off and stepped away from work, focusing on our family fully.

> WHEN I STARTED DELICIOUSLY ELLA I MADE A DECISION TO OPEN UP ABOUT THE MENTAL AND PHYSICAL CHALLENGES I'D BEEN THROUGH WITH MY ILLNESS

June and July passed in a bit of a blur – all I wanted to do was support Matt and it was heart-breaking to see him so distraught. I still loved our mission with Deliciously Ella and cared deeply for our community, but to lead a business you need to be inspired, and under those circumstances it was impossible to see past the pain we were feeling. I was overwhelmed trying to run the business without Matt's full support, as I just didn't have all of the

skills and capabilities to take on elements of his role; and the vulnerability of existing in the public space with the stream of criticism that inevitably comes with that became more challenging than ever before. In the midst of all this, we'd also been renovating our new dream house, selling our flat, moving, packing and managing everything else that goes with it.

As we were getting settled in our new home and enjoying a rare, quiet, joyful moment, we heard some scratching beneath a floorboard. We decided to ignore it, but the next day went into our kitchen to find the remnants of 20 energy balls strewn across the floor. A colony of rats had moved in with us... It felt like we'd been dealt a fairly sizeable number of challenges to cope with at that point, then, just to add to them, one evening when we were back at the house picking up some clothes, Austin trotted out to the patio through a door left open by the builders, and ate a large amount of the rat poison. We had to rush him to an emergency vet and as we sat there watching him have his stomach pumped, we cried and laughed at the same time wondering what had happened to us!

Stress is a crazy thing and something that Matt has always seemingly taken in his stride. Clearly it all had got too much though and, one day, while walking from the office to get himself some lunch, Matt collapsed on the street and was rushed to A & E. He couldn't hold himself up, could barely speak and was projectile vomiting. After five hours or so he started to feel better but was left with dizziness, exhaustion and tinnitus. The doctors thought he had had a problem with his inner ear and sent him home on strict bedrest.

IT FELT LIKE WE'D BEEN DEALT A FAIRLY SIZEABLE NUMBER OF CHALLENGES AT THAT POINT, THEN JUST TO ADD TO THEM, ONE EVENING AUSTIN TROTTED OUT TO THE PATIO AND ATE A LARGE AMOUNT OF RAT POISON

In retrospect, it was pretty obvious that we had been hurtling towards burnout. That summer had been extremely intense and it hadn't been helped by the fact that we had been pushing ourselves so hard before everything unravelled. In 18 months, we'd cancelled five attempts at a holiday, spent a lot of our honeymoon answering work emails and had totally lost sight of the concept of a weekend or a night off. We'd been so excited and challenged by Deliciously Ella that it had become all-consuming. Something clicked and as we lay in bed that night, just feeling so grateful that Matt was okay, we both knew that something had to change. We cancelled everything in our diaries for the following week, turned our phones off, left the team in charge and went to Greece. Throughout six heavenly days we reconnected with ourselves and with each other, and made a real commitment to assess the way we were living and to find a better sense of balance. I'd started Deliciously Ella back in 2012 to help me regain my health and I needed it again now to give us both a push back in the right direction.

From the day we arrived back from our trip, we started leaving our computers in the office (almost) every night, made an effort to book date nights, made time for our friends and got back into the routine of sitting down to a home-cooked meal in the evening. I also went back to my daily yoga practice, which I hadn't made time for in too long. Things with Matt's mum were still difficult and we had to adjust to a new normal, but we had regained a sense of balance in our lives, which we'd sorely missed.

Writing this chapter months later, I'm really proud to say that we've mostly kept up with all our healthy habits and I feel so much better for it. Despite losing my inspiration for a short while, the intense nature of that summer pushed me to reconnect with the roots of Deliciously Ella and why I started it, and I began to feel more passionate about what we do and why than ever before.

PEA AND WATERCRESS SOUP

If you're after something with lots of greens then this is for you! It is a simple soup with just five ingredients: onion, garlic, peas, watercress and veggie stock. If you can't find watercress you can easily swap it for spinach, or add some of that in too.

SERVES 4

olive oil
1 onion, chopped
2 garlic cloves, chopped
600ml boiling water
1 tablespoon vegetable bouillon
    powder or 1 vegetable
    stock cube
300g frozen peas
100g watercress
salt and pepper

Place a pan over a medium heat and add a drizzle of olive oil, the onion, garlic and a pinch of salt and pepper. Cook until soft, about 5–10 minutes. Add the boiling water, bouillon powder (or stock cube) and peas and simmer for another 10 minutes.

Finally, add the watercress and cook for 5 more minutes. Remove from the heat and blend until smooth.

APPLE AND CELERIAC SOUP

This is quite a sweet soup, but I really like that about it. Each sip feels warming and comforting and the subtle hint of allspice works so well with the apples, while the coriander balances the sweet and savoury mix. Soups generally are very easy to make, and with just five ingredients, this one is a perfect option when you're short on time.

SERVES 4

1 celeriac, peeled and diced
2 red apples (Braeburn work best),
    cored, peeled and diced
750ml almond milk
2 teaspoons allspice
2 teaspoons ground coriander
salt and pepper

Place the celeriac and apples in a pan with the rest of the ingredients and cook over a medium heat for about 45–50 minutes until the celeriac and apples are really soft.

Once cooked, remove from the heat and blend until smooth, adding a dash of water as needed until you reach the consistency you like best.

TIP
This soup is delicious served with a handful of sunflower seeds and toasted sourdough bread.

CREAMY MUSHROOM SOUP

I love mushroom soup. There's something about the richness of mushrooms that keeps me coming back for more every time. Adding a little yoghurt makes it thick and creamy, while the thyme gives it a lovely flavour. Depending on the time of year, wild mushrooms can be delicious, so do experiment with seasonal varieties.

SERVES 4

olive oil
1 large onion (about 125g), chopped
2 garlic cloves, chopped
800g chestnut mushrooms (or any other mushrooms you have), roughly chopped
1 tablespoon dried thyme
1 tablespoon vegetable bouillon powder or 1 vegetable stock cube
2 tablespoons plain yoghurt (we use a pure coconut yoghurt), plus extra to garnish
salt and pepper

Place a pan over a medium heat and add a drizzle of olive oil, the onion, garlic and a pinch of salt. Cook until soft, about 5–10 minutes.

Add the mushrooms, thyme and some pepper, cover the pan and leave for 10 minutes until the mushrooms are soft, giving them a stir every now and again. Once the mushrooms are soft, add 1 litre water and the bouillon powder (or stock cube), then bring to the boil before reducing the heat and leaving to simmer for 20–25 minutes.

Once the mushrooms are soft, remove the pan from the heat, add the yoghurt and blend until smooth. Stir through a little extra yoghurt to garnish before serving.

TIP
This soup is delicious topped with a drizzle of olive oil and a handful of toasted hazelnuts.

- Original Granola
  with Raisins, Coconut & Toasted
  seeds

  Nutty Granola
  with Hazelnut, Almond & Cashew

- Bircher Muesli
  with Raspberry & Apple

Gluten & Dairy Free ~ High in fibre
Made with love in the U.K. £3·99

TOMATO AND FENNEL SOUP

This has been one of our most popular soups. Tomato soup is familiar and warming on a cold day, but adding the fennel to this one gives it another layer of flavour, making it a little more interesting. It's delicious served topped with a dollop of coconut yoghurt.

SERVES 4

olive oil
1 red onion, peeled and chopped
1 garlic clove, peeled and
    chopped
3 thyme sprigs, leaves stripped
    and roughly chopped
2 fennel bulbs, sliced
1 tablespoon tomato purée
1 × 400g tin of tomatoes
300g fresh tomatoes
400ml water
1 tablespoon maple syrup
1 teaspoon chilli flakes
salt and pepper

Place a pan over a medium heat and add a drizzle of olive oil, the onion, garlic and a pinch of salt. Cook until soft, about 5–10 minutes.

Add the thyme leaves, fennel and tomato purée and cook for another 10–15 minutes before adding the rest of the ingredients. Bring to the boil before reducing the heat and leaving to simmer for 45–50 minutes until everything is really soft, adding a splash more water if it becomes too thick.

Once cooked, remove from the heat, add some freshly cracked pepper, a pinch more salt, if it needs it, and blend until smooth, adding a dash of water until you reach the consistency you like best.

SOUPER VEG SOUP

This is the ultimate leftovers soup – you can add any veggies you have in your fridge and really up your five-a-day intake at the same time! We've used spinach, broccoli, squash, onion and garlic, as well as a little ginger for flavour and coconut milk for creaminess, but you can mix and match according to what you have. It's been one of our most popular soups and one of my favourites too.

SERVES 4

olive oil
½ butternut squash, peeled,
  deseeded and cut into cubes
  no larger than 1cm
1 red onion, sliced
1 thumb-sized piece of ginger,
  peeled and chopped
2 garlic cloves, chopped
1 head of broccoli, cut
  into florets
770ml coconut milk (from
  a carton)
100g baby spinach
salt

Place a saucepan over a medium heat and add a drizzle of olive oil, the squash, onion, ginger, garlic and a pinch of salt. Cook until soft, about 5–10 minutes. Add the broccoli florets and cook for another 15 minutes.

Once the squash feels soft, add the coconut milk and cook for a final 10 minutes, then stir in the spinach and allow it to wilt.

Remove the soup from the heat and blend until smooth, adding a dash of water until you reach the consistency you like best.

TANDOORI BUTTERNUT SQUASH SOUP

If I'm making soup as part of a meal for friends or a starter for dinner this is one I'll often turn to, especially on cold autumn evenings. Tandoori isn't a common flavour in soups, so it often surprises people, yet it gives this recipe a gentle heat and depth, which is really enhanced by the warming ginger, celery and coriander. I like my soups super creamy and thick but you can adjust the consistency with water to make yours how you like.

SERVES 4

olive oil
1 onion, roughly chopped
1 celery stalk, roughly chopped
1 garlic clove, chopped
1 tablespoon tandoori paste
(see tip)
1 butternut squash, peeled,
deseeded and cut into cubes
no larger than 1cm
2 × 400g tins of coconut milk
1 × 400g tin of butter beans,
drained and rinsed
2 teaspoons ground ginger
1 teaspoon ground coriander
salt and pepper

Place a saucepan over a medium heat and add a drizzle of olive oil, the onion, celery, garlic and a pinch of salt. Cook until soft, about 5–10 minutes.

Once soft, add the tandoori paste and butternut squash and cook for a further 5 minutes before adding the coconut milk, butter beans, ginger, coriander and 500ml water. Bring the whole thing to the boil before reducing the heat and leaving to simmer for 25–30 minutes.

Once everything is soft, remove from the heat and blend until smooth, adding another dash of water until you reach the consistency you like best.

TIP
If you want to make your own tandoori paste, simply place a teaspoon of chilli powder, mustard seeds, fennel seeds, ground coriander, ground turmeric, paprika and salt along with a thumb-sized piece of ginger and 2 tablespoons of lime juice and 2 of tomato purée in a food processor and pulse until a paste has formed.

FIVE-BEAN CHILLI WITH CORN BREAD

I think this has been one of our most requested recipes. I can't begin to count the number of emails I've had asking for it, so I'm really excited to finally share it with you. Both the chilli and the corn bread are surprisingly easy to make and they taste so incredibly good! The chilli is really hearty and I love the texture combination of the beans in the chilli and the crispy crust of the golden corn bread. If you're going to make one recipe in this book then make this!

THE CHILLI SERVES 4; THE CORN BREAD MAKES ENOUGH FOR 10

FOR THE CORN BREAD
750g drained tinned sweetcorn (3–4 tins depending on size)
450ml almond milk
150ml sunflower, rapeseed or vegetable oil
1 tablespoon apple cider vinegar
25g coriander, chopped
1 × 400g tin of black beans, drained and rinsed
2 red chillies, deseeded and finely chopped
1 tablespoon sea salt flakes
pinch of pepper

FOR THE DRY INGREDIENTS
60g plain flour (we use a gluten-free one)
30g rice flour
400g polenta
1 tablespoon corn flour
1 teaspoon baking powder
2 teaspoons bicarbonate of soda

FOR THE FIVE-BEAN CHILLI
olive oil
1 onion, chopped
1 celery stalk, finely chopped
2 garlic cloves, chopped
1 red chilli, deseeded and chopped
1 teaspoon dried rosemary
1 teaspoon dried thyme
3 tablespoons tomato purée
2 × 400g tins of mixed beans
1 × 400g tin of tomatoes
1 tablespoon maple syrup

Start by making the corn bread.

Preheat the oven to 200°C (fan 180°C). Line a deep 35 × 25cm baking tin with baking parchment. Place three quarters of the sweetcorn in a food processor and pulse until smooth. Once smooth, mix together with the rest of the whole sweetcorn kernels.

Place all the dry ingredients in a large mixing bowl and stir well. Once mixed, add the almond milk, oil and apple cider vinegar and give everything another really good stir until well combined. Next, add the coriander, black beans, chilli, salt, pepper and sweetcorn, giving it all one final mix.

Once the mixture has come together, pour into the lined baking tin and bake in the oven for 50–55 minutes until golden and cooked through. To test if it is cooked, insert a knife into the corn bread, it should come out clean. If not, place back in the oven for 5 more minutes to cook through.

While the corn bread is baking, prepare the chilli. Place a large saucepan over a medium heat and add a drizzle of olive oil, the onion, celery, garlic and a pinch of salt and cook until soft, about 5–10 minutes.

recipe continues overleaf

TO SERVE
2 red chillies, sliced
handful of sliced spring onions

Now add the chilli, rosemary, thyme and tomato purée and cook for another 5 minutes. Add the beans, tomatoes, 150ml water, maple syrup and some pepper and bring to the boil, then lower the heat and leave to simmer for 25–30 minutes, at which point it should have a thick consistency.

When you are ready to serve sprinkle the chillies and spring onion over the top and enjoy with the corn bread.

TIPS
The corn bread is best eaten fresh, especially when it's warm out the oven, but the chilli tastes even better the next day, so keep any extra in the fridge to take to work as a packed lunch or pop it in the freezer if you want it to last longer. If you do have leftovers of the corn bread, however, you can store it in an airtight container and enjoy it the next day.

For the mixed beans, we buy tins made up of red kidney beans, black-eyed beans, borlotti beans, lima beans and pea navy beans, but there are different kinds available so just use what you like.

SWEET POTATO AND COURGETTE STEW

While lots of people love sandwiches and salads at lunch, I love having a hot lunch so I make big batches of this for me and Matt at the weekend and then keep the leftovers to heat up at my desk. The sweet potato is so comforting and filling, perfect with some brown rice or quinoa for dinner and some sliced avocado and fresh rocket for lunch.

SERVES 4

2 sweet potatoes, peeled
    and cubed
olive oil
1 onion, sliced
2 garlic cloves, chopped
1 teaspoon ground cumin
1 teaspoon dried coriander
1 teaspoon paprika
½ teaspoon mustard seeds
pinch of chilli flakes
1 × 400g tin of coconut milk
1 × 400g tin of tomatoes
1 tablespoon apple cider vinegar
1 tablespoon maple syrup
1 courgette, halved lengthways
    and cut into half moons
    no more than 1cm-thick
1 × 400g tin of chickpeas,
    drained and rinsed
100g baby spinach
salt

Bring a pan of water to the boil over a medium heat and add the chopped sweet potato. Simmer for 15 minutes, until tender but not too soft (otherwise it will fall apart when cooking later on), before draining.

While the sweet potatoes are cooking, place another saucepan over a medium heat and add a drizzle of olive oil, the onion, garlic and a pinch of salt. Cook for about 5–10 minutes, until soft.

Once soft, add the cumin, coriander, paprika, mustard seeds, chilli flakes and cooked sweet potatoes, and cook for a further 5 minutes before adding the coconut milk, tinned tomatoes, apple cider vinegar and maple syrup. Bring the whole thing to a boil before reducing the temperature and leaving to simmer for 25–30 minutes. Add the courgettes and chickpeas and cook for a further 10–15 minutes until soft.

Once everything is cooked, remove from the heat and stir through the spinach to wilt, adding another dash of water if needed until you reach the consistency you like best.

TIP
This stew is even better left overnight and enjoyed the next day. It's also a great recipe to help you use up any leftover veg – swap the courgettes for veggies like cauliflower, baby corn or mangetout or add them in too.

LENTIL AND POTATO STEW

This hearty lentil and potato stew is brilliant if you want something nourishing and sustaining on cold winter days, packed full of veggie protein. It's simple in flavour with hints of cumin in the stew and a nice sprinkling of fresh parsley stirred through at the end but most of the flavour comes from the veg – onion, carrot, celery, garlic, kale, tomatoes and potatoes, which are simmered with the lentils.

SERVES 4

250g baby potatoes, halved
olive oil
2 onions, sliced
1 large celery stalk, sliced
3 garlic cloves, sliced
1 large carrot, peeled and sliced
1 tablespoon vegetable bouillon powder or 1 vegetable stock cube
2 tablespoons tomato purée
1 teaspoon ground cumin
125g dried green lentils
1 × 400g tin of tomatoes
150g kale, stems removed, leaves roughly chopped
handful of parsley, chopped
salt and pepper

Preheat the oven to 200°C (fan 180°C).

Place the potatoes in a baking tray and drizzle with olive oil. Mix with some salt and pepper then place in the oven for 25–30 minutes until golden. Remove and leave to one side.

While the potatoes are cooking, place the onion, celery, garlic and carrot in a pan with a drizzle of olive oil and cook over a medium heat for 25–30 minutes until soft. Once soft, add the bouillon powder (or stock cube), tomato purée and cumin and cook for 5 minutes more, stirring occasionally to ensure it doesn't stick to the bottom of the pan. Then add the green lentils and cover with water. Bring to the boil, before reducing to a simmer and leaving to cook for another 35–40 minutes or until the lentils are soft.

Once the lentils are soft and the water has reduced to form a stew-like consistency, mix in the roasted potatoes, tinned tomatoes and kale and cook for another 5–10 minutes. Check the seasoning then sprinkle over the parsley before serving.

TIP
We sometimes add pearl onions to this stew, which are delicious but not always that easy to find. If you can get hold of them add 100g to the roasting tray with the potatoes and mix through the stew once it is ready to serve.

TUSCAN BEAN STEW

I absolutely love butter beans, which is why I'm such a fan of this recipe. The garlic and onions are fried with rosemary and thyme before being simmered with the parsnips and plum tomatoes. The sauce has a wonderful rich tomato flavour which is hearty and warming when paired with the creamy beans, and makes this stew perfect for an easy supper at the end of a long day. I serve it with brown rice or toasted sourdough bread.

SERVES 3–4

olive oil
1 red onion, thinly sliced
2 garlic cloves, thinly sliced
1 teaspoon dried thyme
1 teaspoon dried rosemary
2 parsnips, peeled and cut into
    2.5cm chunks
175g plum tomatoes
1 tablespoon tomato purée
1 × 400g tin of butter beans,
    drained and rinsed
2 × 400g tins of tomatoes
salt and pepper
handful of chopped flat-leaf
    parsley, to serve (optional)

Pour a drizzle of olive oil into a heavy-based pan. Add the onion, garlic, rosemary, thyme and a pinch of salt and cook over a medium heat for 5–10 minutes, until the onion is soft.

Once the onion is soft, add the parsnips and plum tomatoes, along with the tomato purée, and cook for another 10–15 minutes, until the tomatoes have collapsed and the parsnips are soft.

Now add the butter beans and tinned tomatoes and give everything a good mix. Bring the liquid to the boil, before reducing the heat and leaving to simmer gently for 10–15 minutes until the tomato sauce is rich and full of flavour. If you have any parsley, sprinkle it over just before serving.

SRI LANKAN CURRY

I cook big curries like this one a lot for my friends and family and they're always a hit. They're also a good way of introducing people to plant-based meals, as a curry feels familiar. This one is a particular favourite, as it's got so many different flavours and textures.

SERVES 4

1 large sweet potato, peeled and cut into bite-sized chunks no bigger than 2.5cm
½ butternut squash, peeled and cut into bite-sized chunks (no bigger than 2.5cm)
3 tablespoons coconut oil
½ teaspoon ground turmeric
½ teaspoon ground cinnamon
½ teaspoon chilli powder
1 teaspoon medium curry powder
2 red peppers, deseeded and sliced
1 teaspoon cumin seeds
1 teaspoon black mustard seeds
1 large red onion, finely sliced
3 garlic cloves, finely sliced
2 green chillies, deseeded and sliced into small pieces (no bigger than 5mm)
1 × 400g tin of coconut milk
1 tablespoon coconut sugar or maple syrup
juice of ½ lime
100g baby spinach
salt

Preheat the oven to 240°C (fan 220°C).

Place the sweet potato and butternut squash in a baking tray with a pinch of salt, 2 tablespoons of the coconut oil, the turmeric, cinnamon, chilli powder and curry powder. Roast in the oven for 30–35 minutes, until soft, adding the sliced pepper for the last 10 minutes. Once ready, remove and leave to one side.

Meanwhile, place a heavy-based pan over a medium heat and the remaining coconut oil. Once hot, add the cumin seeds and black mustard seeds and cook for 30 seconds, until they begin to pop.

Add the red onion, garlic and chilli and cook for another 5 minutes before adding the coconut milk and coconut sugar. Cook for a further 15 minutes, adding the lime juice during the last 5 minutes.

Add the roasted squash, sweet potatoes and peppers and cook for 5 more minutes, stirring continuously to ensure it doesn't stick to the bottom of the pan.

Finally, stir through the spinach and leave to wilt before serving.

TIPS

If you want to mix up the greens, green beans also work really well in this dish either as well as or in place of the spinach.

You could make a double batch of this curry and freeze half for another day. It freezes so well and is really easy to cook straight from the freezer – just place it into an oven set at 200°C (fan 180°C) for 20–25 minutes until cooked through.

GREEN THAI CURRY

Alongside the Five-bean chilli (see page 162–5), this is the deli recipe that we've had the most requests for so I'm really excited to share it. The paste is delicious – the mix of ginger, lemongrass, coriander, cumin, lime, onion and chilli is just a dream. It's then cooked with coconut milk, so each mouthful of this is just bursting with rich flavours. This is always a crowd-pleaser and a nice option for anyone who is a little nervous about vegan cooking, as it feels really familiar.

SERVES 4

FOR THE CURRY PASTE
½ large onion, roughly chopped
1 red chilli, roughly chopped
1 garlic clove, roughly chopped
1 lemongrass stalk, bashed and
   roughly chopped
1 thumb-sized piece of ginger,
   peeled and roughly chopped
handful of coriander (about 20g)
1 teaspoon ground cumin
1 lime leaf
3½ tablespoons coconut oil

FOR THE CURRY
2 red peppers, deseeded and
   cut into bite-sized chunks
2 courgettes, halved
   lengthways and sliced into
   chunky half moons
olive oil
1 tablespoon coconut oil
2 × 400g tins of coconut milk
   (see tip)
1 tablespoon tamari
handful of mangetout (about 50g)
handful of fresh coriander,
   chopped
salt

Preheat the oven to 240°C (fan 220°C).

Place all of the paste ingredients in a food processor and blitz until smooth.

Place the peppers and courgettes in a baking tray with a pinch of salt and a drizzle of olive oil. Roast for 10 minutes until they have lost their raw look but still have a slight crunch, then remove and leave to one side.

Next, place the coconut oil in a heavy-based pan over a medium heat. Once hot, add the curry paste and cook for 5 minutes until soft. Add the coconut milk and tamari and bring to the boil – then lower the heat and simmer for 5 minutes. Remove from the heat and blitz using a hand blender, then pass through a sieve to remove any unwanted bits (if needed). Place back on to a low heat and add the roasted vegetables and mangetout and cook for a final 5 minutes. Try not to overcook this curry – the sauce only needs this short cooking time and there is a chance it could form a layer of oil on top if you cook it for longer and reduce it too much.

Sprinkle with some chopped coriander to serve.

TIP
It's really important to use thick, creamy coconut milk in this recipe. We use a brand called Chaokoh – but if you can't find that you can just use a good-quality one. Make sure to give the milk a good mix before using – you can do this using a hand whisk or a stand mixer.

YELLOW THAI CURRY

Aubergines are one of my favourite ingredients to use in a curry as they soak up all of the flavours like a sponge. I've lost count of how many bowls of this curry I've eaten in the last few years; when I'm having a busy week I pop into the deli and devour a bowl with brown rice – it's warming, hearty and always keeps me going for hours. This one also happens to be one of Matt's favourites too.

SERVES 4

FOR THE CURRY PASTE
½ large onion, roughly chopped
1 red chilli, roughly chopped
1 garlic clove, roughly chopped
1 thumb-sized piece of ginger, peeled and roughly chopped
1 teaspoon ground coriander
1 teaspoon ground cumin
1 teaspoon ground turmeric
1 lemongrass stalk, bashed and roughly chopped
1 lime leaf
3½ tablespoons coconut oil

FOR THE CURRY
2 red peppers, deseeded and cut into bite-sized chunks
1 large aubergine, cut into bite-size pieces
100g button mushrooms
100g baby corn, cut in half
olive oil
1 tablespoon coconut oil
2 × 400g tins of coconut milk (see tip on page 174)
1 tablespoon tamari
handful of Thai basil, roughly chopped
salt

Preheat the oven to 240°C (fan 220°C).

Place all of the paste ingredients in a food processor and blitz until smooth.

Place the peppers, aubergine, mushrooms and baby corn in a baking tray with a little olive oil and salt. Roast in the oven for 10–15 minutes, so that they take on a bit of colour, then remove and leave to one side.

Next, place the coconut oil in a heavy-based pan over a medium heat. Once hot, add the curry paste and cook for 5 minutes until soft. Add the coconut milk and tamari and bring to the boil – then lower the heat and simmer for 5 minutes. Remove from the heat and blitz using a hand blender, then pass through a sieve to remove any unwanted bits (if needed). Place back on to a medium heat and add the roasted vegetables, then cook for a final 5 minutes. Try not to overcook this curry – the sauce only needs this short cooking time and there is a chance it could form a layer of oil on top if you cook it for longer and reduce it too much.

Once everything is cooked through, sprinkle with a handful of chopped Thai basil.

TIP
You could make a double batch of this curry and freeze half for another day. It freezes so well and is really easy to cook straight from the freezer – just place it into an oven set at 200°C (fan 180°C) for 20–25 minutes until cooked through.

FENNEL AND AUBERGINE CURRY

This is a lovely simple dish – it's just roasted aubergine and fennel, cooked until golden, then simmered with onions, ginger, chopped chilli and garlic, tomatoes and garam masala – eight ingredients and very little prep.

SERVES 4

1 large aubergine, cut into
    bite-sized chunks
olive oil
1 fennel bulb, cut into
    bite-sized chunks
1 onion, finely sliced
2 garlic cloves, finely sliced
1 red chilli, finely sliced
1 tablespoon ground ginger
2 × 400g tins of tomatoes
1 teaspoon garam masala
salt and pepper

Preheat the oven to 240°C (fan 220°C).

Place the aubergine in a baking tray, along with a little olive oil and some salt and pepper. Roast in the oven for 35–40 minutes until golden, adding the fennel for the last 10–15 minutes.

While the aubergines and fennel are cooking, place the onion, garlic, chilli and ginger in a heavy-based pan along with a drizzle of olive oil and a pinch of salt. Cook over a medium heat for 5–10 minutes, until soft.

Now add the garam masala and cook for a further 5 minutes before adding the tinned tomatoes, fennel and aubergine. Bring everything to the boil, then lower the heat to a simmer and cook for 50–55 minutes until really soft, adding more water if it gets too thick.

CAULIFLOWER AND RED LENTIL DHAL

This dhal has remained one of my staples for the last few years. Everyone loves it and I couldn't recommend it more. It feels really creamy and the mix of spices creates such a depth of flavour, while the apricots add something a little unusual, as well as a nice sweetness.

SERVES 4

2 teaspoons coconut oil
1 onion, roughly chopped
2 carrots, peeled and chopped
2 garlic cloves, chopped
2 teaspoons medium
    curry powder
1 teaspoon smoked paprika
1 teaspoon mustard seeds
200g split red lentils
handful of dried apricots
    (about 6), chopped
1 × 400g tin of coconut milk
3 tablespoons coconut milk or
    almond milk (from a carton)
1 cauliflower, cut into florets
olive oil
handful of baby spinach
    (optional)
salt and pepper

Preheat the oven to 240°C (fan 220°C).

Put the coconut oil into a large saucepan over a medium heat. Add the onion, carrots, garlic and a pinch of salt and cook until soft, around 15 minutes.

Add the curry powder, paprika and mustard seeds and cook for a further 5 minutes, before adding the lentils and apricots. Mix well and cover with the tinned coconut milk, stirring to stop it catching and burning. If needed, keep adding a dash of coconut or almond milk from a carton until the lentils are cooked through and the consistency is thick and a little sticky, about 30–35 minutes.

While this cooks, roast your cauliflower. Put the cauliflower florets into a baking tray with a drizzle of olive oil and some salt and pepper and roast for 8 minutes. Remove and add the florets to the lentils and cook for a further 5–10 minutes – you want the cauliflower to be cooked but still have a little bite.

Finally, add the spinach, if using, and leave it to wilt before serving.

TIP
This dhal is also delicious with a teaspoon of ground cardamom and ½ teaspoon of cloves, if you like these flavours. You can also sprinkle a handful of toasted almonds over the top for a delicious crunch.

SWEET

The Deliciously Ella Diary
— *part 5*

In some ways, Deliciously Ella has changed a lot since I started it in my kitchen back in 2012, yet in many ways nothing has changed: my main role and focus is to connect and engage with our community and I still spend a lot of my day doing that. One of the biggest shifts has been taking on the most unbelievable team, which has given us such strength and allowed me and Matt to take a step back from the day-to-day operations so that we can focus on being creative, bringing innovation to what we do and, most importantly, being fully connected to you. It also means that now, more than ever, Deliciously Ella is a collective voice. We've gradually shifted from being something deeply personal and focused on a specific health issue, to something that can act as a tool or a resource for anyone, no matter what their dietary preferences. In this chapter, I wanted to share my thoughts on that evolution and what we stand for now.

When I first started my blog, the outlook of Deliciously Ella was very insular. I wrote for myself and that remained true even as the first readers joined. The primary focus was getting my own health back on track and finding interesting ways to eat better so that I would stay inspired. At that point, the site should really have been called ellawoodward.com but I think I was subconsciously afraid of the judgement and the opinions of those around me when I confessed to writing a blog, particularly as I lacked key competencies both in IT and the culinary world, so I took my surname away to make it more anonymous. But as the audience grew, I knew that I had to make the site more relevant to anyone looking to increase the plant-based meals in their life and my focus shifted. I stopped sharing the personal anecdotes and snippets

of what I was researching. I simultaneously started thinking about what the audience wanted, what was seasonal and relevant to that week, and analysing what people were engaging in. Yet despite dropping a bit of the personal side, much of our audience continued to see me as 'Deliciously Ella', rather than that being the brand, and to some extent it became an alter ego. Every time I was stopped in the street or asked for a photo, people said, 'Are you Deliciously Ella?', never 'Are you Ella Mills/Woodward?' (I changed my name to Mills after we got married). With this came a sense that everything I ever did, made or said was Instagram-ready and as I started to realise that I became increasingly uncomfortable with it. It has become clear that the line between Ella Mills – me, a normal, completely imperfect human being – and the shinier world of Deliciously Ella has become very blurred. This blurring, coupled with the fact that Deliciously Ella has had a lot of media attention (some of which has been good and some not-so-much), has meant that what we're about has become pretty confused.

FROM DAY ONE DELICIOUSLY ELLA HAS BEEN ABOUT CELEBRATING FRUITS, VEGETABLES AND NATURAL WHOLE FOODS, AND TURNING THEM INTO SOMETHING EXCITING

The foundation of what we do has remained the same throughout our journey. From day one Deliciously Ella has been about celebrating fruit, vegetables and natural whole foods, and turning those simple ingredients into something exciting. My very first blog posts were for dishes like cinnamon and paprika sweet potato wedges, avocado cream and aubergine salads, admittedly things have got a little more interesting from there and it's now about vegan versions of shakshuka, creative veggie salads and different types of dhal. This is the approach we took at the deli too, as our number one aim there was to use the space to show people that eating plant-based food didn't have to be weird or ostentatious, it could

be deliciously simple. We wanted our dishes to look familiar and all of our ingredient lists to be natural and uncomplicated. I felt that as the world of healthy eating had exploded, so had the association that it had to be complicated and use ingredients that were hard to come by. I opened my Instagram feed too many times to see adaptogenic mushroom lattes and other innovative ideas,

WE ADD EXTRA SPARKLE
BECAUSE, LET'S BE
HONEST, BROCCOLI DOES
SOMETIMES NEED TO BE
JAZZED UP A LITTLE AS
MANY PEOPLE AREN'T
OVERLY EXCITED ABOUT
EATING THEIR GREENS

and worried that others would feel they couldn't take inspiration from the healthy space, as it could appear too niche, too expensive and too confusing. As I said in the Introduction, I had a more regimented approach when I first started and was more drawn to some of these weird and wonderful ingredients, as I was very unwell and was trying to remedy that. I saw such incredible benefits from changing my diet that I wanted to share that with the world. However, this wasn't to the extent that everyone should do as I did – the idea was just that readers take some inspiration and ideas to incorporate elements into their own lives. As things at Deliciously Ella got busier my personal interest shifted to what worked in my schedule, which tended to be simpler things, and as the audience grew I wanted everything to feel more accessible. My goal became to get everyone excited about the humble little chickpea, carrots, potatoes, herbs, spices and things that we can all access relatively easily, which I hope is what this book does.

The same goes with the types of flours and grains we use now. To begin with I went completely gluten-free, as I was reacting to it and this did really help my digestive issues, but as my health stabilised I started including things like rye, sourdough and spelt into my diet again and really enjoyed cooking with them so we started using them in the deli too. You'll find our favourite spelt muffins, for example, in our breakfast chapter (see pages 47, 50 and 53) – but you can easily swap the spelt flour for something that is gluten-free, if that works better for you.

Ultimately, our goals and what we stand for as a community are pretty simple, and my biggest frustration is that these get overcomplicated and subsequently criticised. There has never been, and never will be, any requirement for anyone to eat fresh plant-based meals three times a day, 365 days a year, but we all know we need to eat more vegetables and all we want to do is get you excited about them. I was recently asked whether I ever just eat toast for dinner, and that summed up where the confusion comes in: yes, of course I eat

toast for dinner sometimes – normally slathered in hummus and black pepper, or smashed avocado with lemon juice, but sometimes just dipped in olive oil – and it definitely doesn't look as beautiful as the images you see on our Instagram feed. I don't post the late-night image of my rye and olive oil because it's not very interesting and it's not going to give anyone new ideas or spark an interest in eating more veg. What we share from Deliciously Ella, as a brand/community/space of inspiration, is never going to be a blow-by-blow account of my day as Ella Mills. I can promise you that wouldn't be very interesting, and most of it would just be of our dog, long days at my computer and bowls of leftovers from recipe testing. We add extra sparkle to inspire people because, let's be honest, broccoli does sometimes need to be jazzed up a little! That doesn't mean, however, that all you should eat is broccoli or that every meal needs to look photogenic and Instagram-ready.

So, make it work for you, enjoy every bite of every meal, eat some more broccoli, find creative ways to get your five-a-day, don't over-complicate healthy and find the balance that works for you: at Deliciously Ella that's what we all believe in.

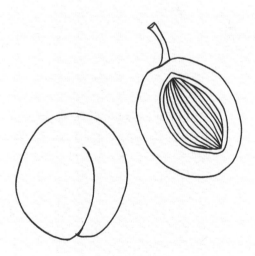

PEANUT COOKIES

When we made these cookies in the office for the first time they got an exceptionally good response, with lots of the team saying they were the best thing we'd ever made! They're really simple, with just six ingredients and they have almost no prep involved, so they're ideal if you need a great treat in a hurry. Then when we launched our packets of peanut butter energy balls we decided to mark the occasion at the deli by running specials made from peanut butter. These cookies were a highlight: we turned them into a cookie sandwich by spreading them with a chocolate ganache, so if you want to do something extra special with yours try adding the ganache below – it's amazing!

MAKES 10

150g porridge oats
100g smooth peanut butter
35g brown rice flour
50ml maple syrup
60g coconut oil, melted
50g coconut sugar

FOR THE GANACHE (OPTIONAL)
2 tablespoons cacao powder
2 tablespoons maple syrup
100g smooth peanut butter
6 tablespoons almond milk

Preheat the oven to 190°C (fan 170°C). Line a large baking tray with baking parchment.

Place all the cookie ingredients in a large bowl and mix until well combined. Use an ice-cream scoop or large spoon to scoop balls of the mixture on to the prepared tray, pushing them down a little to form cookie shapes.

Bake in the oven for 10–15 minutes, until golden. Remove and leave to cool a little before enjoying.

If you want to turn these peanut cookies into sandwiches (see above), place all of the ganache ingredients in a small pan and heat until they come together to form a paste. Once very thick, remove from the heat and leave to cool. When cool, place the ganache into a piping bag and pipe equal amounts on to five of the cookies, before placing another cookie on top of each.

TIP
If you don't like peanuts or just fancy changing these up, then switch the peanut butter for almond or cashew butter.

ALMOND VICTORIA CAKE

We've made this cake to celebrate team birthdays at our office more times than I can remember and everyone loves it. It used to be called a MaE cake in the deli, so if you're looking for that recipe this is it! I know lots of people get worried about baking cakes, and think they're not natural 'bakers' but the brilliant thing about vegan cake mixes is that they are so simple to make: the ingredients all just get stirred together and there's no need for complicated beating or whisking.

There is quite a lot of maple syrup in this cake but that's because it's really for a special occasion, rather than an everyday bake. If you do want to make a version with less syrup, you can change the quantity of buckwheat flour to 250g, the maple syrup to 300ml and the almond milk to 240ml – it's still delicious, but less sweet and indulgent.

SERVES 12

FOR THE CAKE
300g ground almonds
240g buckwheat flour
    (or plain flour)
1 tablespoon bicarbonate
    of soda
pinch of sea salt flakes
440ml maple syrup
100ml almond milk
the water from 1 × 400g tin
    of chickpeas (not the
    chickpeas themselves)

FOR THE ICING
400g pure coconut yoghurt
    (see tip on page 211)
50ml maple syrup
the scraped seeds of 1 vanilla
    pod or 1 teaspoon
    vanilla powder

FOR THE MIDDLE
100g strawberry jam

TO DECORATE (OPTIONAL)
handful of fresh strawberries,
    chopped
handful of edible flowers

Preheat the oven to 200°C (fan 180°C). Line two 23cm cake tins with baking parchment.

In a large bowl, mix the ground almonds, buckwheat flour, bicarb and salt, stirring well to remove any lumps. Add the maple syrup, almond milk and chickpea water and mix again until it comes together to form a smooth batter.

Pour equal amounts of the batter into the lined tins and bake for 20 minutes, until well risen and a knife inserted in the centre comes out clean – if it doesn't, place the tins back in the oven for 5 more minutes. Once ready, remove and leave the cakes to cool in their tins until room temperature, around 30 minutes.

While the cakes cool, make the icing. Whisk the coconut yoghurt using an electric whisk – either a stand mixer or a hand whisk – until it becomes really thick, around 5–10 minutes. It's really important to whisk the yoghurt on its own first, before adding the maple syrup. Once it feels very thick and holds its shape, add the syrup and vanilla and continue whisking for a further minute. If you don't have an electric whisk you can use a balloon whisk – just make sure you whisk long enough to get a good amount of air and thickness into the mix.

Once the cakes are cool, spread the jam over one and sandwich it with the other. Spoon the icing over the top of the cake and smooth it over evenly. We like adding berries and edible flowers as decoration.

CARROT CAKE

I love carrot cake, it's rich and comforting and in this recipe the burst of juicy raisins and the coconut sugar bring out the natural sweetness of the carrots. We use an icing made from cashew nuts, as we think they're a great match for the flavours in the cake, but the coconut yoghurt icing on page 190 also works well.

SERVES 10

FOR THE CAKE
400g buckwheat flour
    (or plain flour)
1 teaspoon bicarbonate of soda
2 teaspoons baking powder
200g ground almonds
400g coconut sugar
3 medium carrots (about 250g),
    peeled and grated
100g raisins
600ml almond milk
100g coconut oil, melted

FOR THE ICING
250g cashews, soaked overnight
    (or for at least 4 hours)
    then drained
7 tablespoons maple syrup
2 tablespoons almond milk
1 teaspoon ground cinnamon

TO SERVE (OPTIONAL)
handful of walnuts (about 30g),
    toasted (see page 35)
    and chopped

Preheat the oven to 200°C (fan 180°C). Line two 23cm cake tins with baking parchment.

In a large bowl, mix together the flour, bicarb, baking powder, ground almonds and coconut sugar, stirring well to remove any lumps. Once combined, add the carrots, raisins, almond milk and coconut oil, and stir again until a batter has formed.

Pour the batter into the lined tins and bake for 35–40 minutes, until well risen and a knife inserted in the centre comes out clean – if it doesn't, place the tins back in the oven for 5 more minutes. Once ready, remove and leave the cakes to cool in their tins until room temperature, about 30 minutes.

While the cakes cool, make the icing. Place the drained cashews in a food processor with the rest of the ingredients and blitz until smooth, about 10–15 minutes – it should be thick enough to hold its shape but thin enough to smooth over a cake. Add another splash of almond milk if it gets too thick.

Remove the cooled cakes from their tins. Spread half of the icing over one cake to make the cake's filling then sandwich the two cakes together. Smooth the other half of the icing over the top, then scatter with the chopped walnuts, if using, and serve.

ORANGE AND BLUEBERRY CAKE

This cake is definitely the most colourful and, I think, the best-looking recipe in this chapter. The orange jam looks amazing as it oozes out the middle, while the fresh blueberries and orange zest bring a vibrancy to the top.

SERVES 12

FOR THE DRY INGREDIENTS
375g ground almonds
110g brown rice flour
    (or plain flour)
2 teaspoons bicarbonate of soda
pinch of sea salt flakes

FOR THE WET INGREDIENTS
the water from 1 × 400g tin
    of chickpeas (not the
    chickpeas themselves)
juice of 1 orange
250ml maple syrup
3 teaspoons apple cider vinegar
1 teaspoon vanilla powder
    (optional)

FOR THE ORANGE JAM
65ml orange juice (the juice
    of 3 oranges)
75ml maple syrup
1 tablespoon arrowroot

FOR THE ICING
200g cashews, soaked overnight
    (or for at least 4 hours)
    then drained
5 tablespoons maple syrup
2 tablespoons almond milk
grated zest of 1 orange

TO FINISH
grated zest of 1 orange
handful of blueberries
    (about 70g)

Preheat the oven to 200°C (fan 180°C). Line two 23cm cake tins with baking parchment.

Place all of the dry ingredients in a bowl and mix well to remove any lumps. Once combined, add the wet ingredients and whisk until the mixture forms a cake batter.

Divide the batter between the lined cake tins and bake for 30 minutes, until a knife inserted in the centre comes out clean – if it doesn't, place the tins back in the oven for 5 more minutes. Once ready, remove and leave the cakes to cool in their tins until room temperature, about 30 minutes.

While the cakes bake, make the orange jam. Place all the ingredients in a small pan over a medium heat and bring to the boil, then lower the heat and leave the liquid to simmer for 10–15 minutes, until it thickens – it should be able to coat the back of a spoon for a couple of seconds before running off. At this point, remove the jam from the heat and leave to cool.

Next, make the icing. Place the drained cashews in a food processor with the rest of the ingredients and blitz until smooth, about 10–15 minutes – it should be thick enough to hold its shape but thin enough to smooth over a cake. Add another splash of almond milk if it gets too thick.

Once the cakes are cool, spoon the orange jam on to one cake, spreading it out to cover the whole surface, then place the other cake on top. Spoon the cashew icing on to the surface of the cake and smooth it around evenly. Finish the cake by sprinkling over the grated orange zest and a handful of blueberries.

PEANUT BUTTER SLICES

An almond, date and oat base topped with a sticky, sweet peanut middle and finished with a creamy chocolate topping, these slices are very indulgent and delicious, which is always a winner in our house. We've had so many emails asking for this recipe, so for all of you who wrote to us here it is.

MAKES 18

FOR THE BASE
200g Medjool dates, pitted
75g porridge oats
2 tablespoons cacao powder
120g flaked almonds

FOR THE MIDDLE LAYER
150g Medjool dates, pitted
350g smooth peanut butter
50ml coconut milk (from a carton)

FOR THE TOP LAYER
85ml maple syrup
10g cacao butter
2 tablespoons cacao powder
handful of peanuts, roughly
  chopped

Line a 29 × 18cm baking tray with baking parchment.

Start by making the base. Place the dates in a food processor and pulse until a paste has formed. Add the oats and cacao powder and pulse until well combined. Finally, add the flaked almonds and give it a final pulse to mix them through. Spread the mixture out in the prepared tray and leave in the fridge to set for 10–15 minutes, until firm.

Make the middle layer by placing the dates in a food processor and pulsing until a paste has formed. Add the peanut butter and coconut milk and pulse until smooth. Spread the mixture over the base and leave to set in the fridge for 30 minutes.

Finally, make the topping by placing the maple syrup, cacao butter and powder in a small pan over a low heat. Heat until the cacao butter has melted, around 5–10 minutes. Pour the mixture over the peanut butter layer and use a spatula to spread it out evenly. Leave to set in the fridge for 1–2 hours, sprinkling a handful of chopped peanuts over the top after about 1 hour, when it is quite firm but before it has fully set.

When ready, lift the set mixture out the baking tray and cut into slices or squares.

TIP
If you don't like peanuts, you can use another nut butter for the middle layer – almond or cashew butter both work well.

MINI APPLE CRUMBLES

These are the sweetest little treat and they taste so delicious when they're warm, straight out the oven. Try serving them as little afternoon tea bites or with a dollop of coconut or cashew ice cream for dessert.

MAKES 12

FOR THE PASTRY
240g ground almonds
170g buckwheat flour
80g coconut oil, plus a little extra, melted, for greasing
8 tablespoons coconut sugar
8 tablespoons almond milk
pinch of sea salt

FOR THE CRUMBLE TOPPING
2 tablespoons buckwheat flour
2 tablespoons coconut sugar

FOR THE FILLING
150g apple purée (we use the Biona brand, or make our own – see tip below)
120ml maple syrup
30g coconut oil
1 teaspoon ground cinnamon
2 teaspoons arrowroot
squeeze of lime juice

Make the pastry by placing all of the pastry ingredients in a food processor and pulsing until a dough forms. Roll the pastry into a ball and chill in the fridge for 30 minutes. If you're making your own apple purée for the filling – now's a good time to get this done.

Preheat the oven to 200°C (fan 180°C). Using a little melted coconut oil, grease a 12-hole muffin tray or 12 silicone moulds.

Remove the pastry from the fridge. Measure out 100g and put this back into the fridge. Roll the rest of the pastry out on a floured work surface until about 1cm thick. Cut it into circle shapes using a 10cm cookie cutter and place in the moulds. Bake in the oven for 10 minutes, until golden, then remove and leave to cool.

Make the topping by putting all of the crumble ingredients into a large bowl, along with the reserved pastry. Rub them together using your fingertips until there are no lumps.

Finally, make the filling by placing all the ingredients in a pan over a medium heat for 10 minutes until smooth and heated through. Spoon equal amounts into the pastry cases and top with a tablespoon of the crumble.

Bake in the oven for 10–15 minutes until golden and delicious.

TIP
If you want to make your own apple purée, simply peel, core and slice 3 eating apples (we use something like a Braeburn) and place them in a pan over a medium heat. Cover with water and cook for 20–25 minutes, until soft. Once soft, drain, add 2 tablespoons of maple syrup – or sweeten to your taste – and blend to form a purée.

FUDGY BROWNIES

I've been so excited to share this recipe with you, it's our all-time favourite and probably the most popular sweet recipe we've ever had at the deli! The brownies are so gooey and fudgy and I love the crunchy bites of walnuts on top. I often make these for friends, serving them hot out the oven with a scoop of coconut ice cream on top.

MAKES 15

1 tablespoon chia seeds
250g buckwheat flour
1 teaspoon bicarbonate of soda
pinch of sea salt
60g cacao powder
330g coconut sugar
100ml almond milk
130g coconut oil, melted
handful of walnuts, chopped

Preheat the oven to 190°C (fan 170°C). Line a 25 × 18 × 4cm baking tin with baking parchment.

Place the chia seeds in a bowl with 4 tablespoons water, mix well then leave to one side for 10 minutes to thicken up.

Place the flour, bicarb, salt, cacao powder and coconut sugar into a large bowl and mix well to remove any lumps. Next, add the almond milk, chia mixture and melted coconut oil and mix well for 5–6 minutes to ensure everything is well combined.

Pour the mixture into the lined tin and sprinkle with the walnuts. Bake for 25–30 minutes, until cooked through but still a little fudgy in the middle. Leave to cool in the tin for 10 minutes, then transfer to a wire rack, before cutting into brownies.

TIP
In the deli we bake these brownies in individual moulds, which gives them a crusty edge, but here we've suggested baking them in one large tray as it's easier and makes them extra gooey.

GIANT PEANUT BUTTER CUPS

We go for a packet of our Nutty Granola to make the base of these treats as it keeps things nice and simple and gives them a deliciously crunchy texture and an extra nutty flavour, but you could use any granola you like. The peanut layer is thick and creamy and the chocolate on top sets to give the cups a firm bite. The combination is incredible.

MAKES 10

FOR THE BASE
280g granola (we use the Deliciously Ella Nutty Granola but you could use any you like – shop-bought or home-made; just make sure it doesn't have any dried fruit in)
50g coconut oil, melted

FOR THE PEANUT LAYER
200g smooth peanut butter
50g coconut sugar
1 teaspoon arrowroot

FOR THE TOPPING
140ml maple syrup
200g cacao butter
50g cacao powder

Blitz the granola and melted coconut oil together in a food processor until smooth. Spoon the mixture into 10 cupcake cases and neatly press down to even out the layer before placing in the fridge.

While the bases are chilling, place all the ingredients for the peanut layer in a small pan over a medium heat and cook until the ingredients are combined, about 5 minutes. Remove from the heat and leave to cool a little, about 10 minutes.

Finally, put all of the topping ingredients into a small pan and melt slowly, over a low heat, until smooth. Once smooth, remove from the heat and stir continuously to ensure the maple and cacao combine thoroughly. Leave to one side to cool for about 5 minutes.

You are now ready to assemble the peanut butter cups. Place a tablespoon of the peanut butter mixture on to the middle of each base, leaving a small gap around the edges or pushing it all the way to the sides if you want to see the peanut butter layer clearly. Then pour over the chocolate topping so that each cup is completely covered. Place in the fridge to set for 1–2 hours.

TIP
Feel free to swap the peanut butter for any other kind of nut butter you like. And if you can't have nuts these work with tahini or sunflower seed butter too.

MANGO AND COCONUT FLAPJACK

We had these chewy flapjacks on the menu when we first opened and I lived off them; they were my main sustenance when things were really busy as I could just grab one as I ran around! For me these are a perfect mid-afternoon snack – sweet but not overly indulgent and I like the fruity element.

MAKES 16

200g dried mango
4 tablespoons coconut oil,
    melted
250g jumbo oats
200g sultanas (or raisins)
4 tablespoons maple syrup
1 tablespoon desiccated coconut

Preheat the oven to 200°C (fan 180°C). Line a 20 × 20cm baking tin with baking parchment.

Soak the mango in boiling water for 10 minutes. After 10 minutes, drain and place in a food processor and blitz until a coarse paste forms. Add the coconut oil, oats, sultanas and maple syrup, and pulse for a few more minutes to bring the mixture together. Finally, add the desiccated coconut and pulse quickly to mix through.

Press the mixture into the lined tin and bake for 20–25 minutes, until golden. Remove from the oven and leave to cool in the tin.

Once completely cool, cut the flapjack into equal squares and store in an airtight container for up to a week.

APPLE AND RASPBERRY SLICES

These apple and raspberry slices are so moreish: they're sweet and a little crumbly. I love them with a turmeric or matcha latte in the afternoon, especially when they're still warm from the oven.

MAKES 16

300g ground almonds
240g buckwheat flour
1 tablespoon bicarbonate of soda
1 tablespoon cacao powder
pinch of sea salt
320ml maple syrup
100ml almond milk
100g apple purée (see tip on page 199)
the water from 1 × 400g tin of chickpeas (not the chickpeas themselves)
2 red apples (we use Braeburn)
100g fresh raspberries

Preheat the oven to 200°C (fan 180°C). Line a 29 × 18 baking tin with baking parchment.

In a large bowl, mix together the ground almonds, buckwheat flour, bicarb, cacao powder and salt, giving it all a good stir to remove any lumps. When the mixture is well combined, add the maple syrup, almond milk, apple purée and chickpea water, mixing well until it comes together to form a batter. Once combined, pour the batter into the lined tin.

Cut the apples in half and remove their core, then slice them thinly into half moons. Place the slices on top of the cake mixture and sprinkle over the raspberries. Bake in the oven for 45–50 minutes or until a knife inserted into the centre comes out clean – if it doesn't, place the tins back in the oven for 5 more minutes. Once ready, remove and leave to cool in the tin.

Once completely cool, lift out the tin and cut into slices, ensuring each slice has some fruit on it.

RED VELVET CUPCAKES

I made these for my niece's first birthday, and the whole family loved them. I think the raspberry-flavoured pink icing is stunning and they taste just as amazing as they look.

MAKES 12

4 tablespoons beetroot powder
1 teaspoon bicarbonate of soda
1 teaspoon baking powder
280g buckwheat flour
200g coconut sugar
300ml almond milk
130ml rapeseed oil
handful of raspberries or
    edible flowers, to decorate
    (optional)

FOR THE ICING
15g freeze-dried raspberries,
    plus a few extra to decorate
400g pure coconut yoghurt
    (see tip)
1 tablespoon maple syrup

Preheat the oven to 190°C (fan 170°C). Line a 12-hole muffin tray with cupcake cases.

Place the beetroot powder, bicarb, baking powder, buckwheat flour and coconut sugar in a large mixing bowl and stir well to remove any lumps. Once combined, add the almond milk and rapeseed oil and stir again until you have a smooth batter.

Pour the batter into the cupcake cases and bake in the oven for 20–25 minutes until well risen and a knife inserted in the centre comes out clean, if not leave to bake for a further 5 minutes. Once ready, remove the cakes from the tray and leave to cool to room temperature on a wire rack.

Meanwhile, place the freeze-dried raspberries in a pestle and mortar and crush to a dust. Next, place the coconut yoghurt in a large mixing bowl and whisk until thick, about 10–15 minutes. Once thick, stir through the maple syrup and freeze-dried raspberry dust and place in the fridge to firm up for around 1 hour.

Once the cupcakes are at room temperature, either spoon on the icing and smooth it with the back of the spoon, or use a piping bag fitted with a 16mm nozzle to pipe it on. Sprinkle with the extra freeze-dried raspberries and a handful of fresh raspberries or edible flowers, if using.

TIPS
Pure coconut yoghurt whips really well. I use the COYO brand as the consistency comes out perfectly but if you can't get hold of coconut yoghurt, mix a really thick plain yoghurt with the raspberry powder and maple syrup and spread it over the top.

If you don't have freeze-dried raspberries you can leave them out of the icing and have it plain, it still tastes delicious.

COFFEE CAKE

This is Matt's favourite cake: it has a fantastically rich coffee flavour and a thick, fluffy icing. It's a perfect weekend afternoon treat and a really lovely recipe to bake as it makes the whole house smell wonderful. It also makes a delicious breakfast without the icing. Simply make up half the amount of batter and bake in a lined 900g loaf tin for 30–35 minutes, then sprinkle with a handful of walnuts.

SERVES 12

3 tablespoons instant
    coffee granules
2 tablespoons boiling water
250g buckwheat flour
    (or plain flour)
200g brown rice flour
200g ground almonds
2 teaspoons bicarbonate of soda
2 teaspoons baking powder
400g coconut sugar
600ml almond milk
100ml rapeseed oil

FOR THE ICING
800g pure coconut yoghurt
    (see tip)
5 tablespoons maple syrup
1 teaspoon cacao powder

Preheat the oven to 200°C (fan 180°C). Line two 23cm cake tins with baking parchment.

Place the coffee granules in a small bowl and stir through the boiling water until dissolved.

In a large bowl, mix together the flours, ground almonds, bicarb, baking powder and coconut sugar, stirring well to remove any lumps. Once combined, add the coffee mixture, almond milk and rapeseed oil, and stir again until a batter has formed. Pour the batter into the tins and bake in the oven for 30–35 minutes until well risen and a knife inserted in the centre comes out clean. If not return the tins to the oven for 5 minutes more. Once ready, remove and leave the cakes to cool in their tins until they reach room temperature, about 30 minutes.

While the cakes cool, make the icing. Whisk the coconut yoghurt using an electric hand whisk (or use a stand mixer) until it becomes really thick and holds itself in peaks, around 5–10 minutes depending on how powerful your whisk is. It is really important to whisk the yoghurt on its own, before adding the maple syrup. When it's thick enough, add the syrup and cacao, and continue whisking for a further minute. If you don't have an electric whisk you can use a balloon whisk – just make sure you whisk long enough to get a good amount of air into the mixture so that it thickens.

Once the cakes are cool, spoon half of the icing over one and sandwich it with the other, then smooth the rest over the top.

TIP
Pure coconut yoghurt whips really well. I use the COYO brand as the consistency comes out perfectly. If you can't get hold of coconut yoghurt, mix a really thick plain yoghurt with the cacao powder and maple syrup and spread it over the top.

ALMOND AND BLUEBERRY COOKIES

Cookies are such an easy and quick thing to bake and this is one of my favourite recipes. They've been a real hit with our team too – the perfect pick-me-up to get us through a long afternoon of emails and planning. We've also made these with chocolate chips instead of the berries, which was delicious, so definitely try that too.

MAKES 10

100g smooth almond butter
40g ground almonds
50ml maple syrup
150g brown rice flour
4 heaped tablespoons coconut
    oil, melted
50g coconut sugar
50g fresh or frozen blueberries

Preheat the oven to 190°C (fan 170°C). Line a large baking tray with baking parchment.

Place all of the ingredients, apart from the blueberries, in a large bowl and mix until well combined. Once combined, gently stir through the blueberries trying not to let them break and burst.

Using an ice cream scoop or large spoon, scoop balls of the mixture on to the lined tray, then press them down a little bit to form a cookie shape.

Bake for 10–15 minutes, until golden. Remove from the oven and leave to cool on the tray. Enjoy either warm or at room temperature.

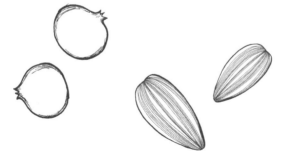

TIP
You can adjust the quantity of blueberries, adding more or less depending on how fruity you want your cookies to be. If you don't have any blueberries, you could add any type of dried fruit, chopped nuts or pieces of dark chocolate.

LEMON CAKE

While Matt will always go for our Coffee cake (see page 211), if I'm in need of a slice of cake, this is the one I'll head for. The lemon jam in the middle is wonderfully sticky, while the icing is light and fluffy and the whole cake has a slight tartness that I adore.

SERVES 12

300g ground almonds
100g brown rice flour
    (or plain flour)
1 teaspoon bicarbonate of soda
½ teaspoon baking powder
grated zest and juice of 1 lemon
300ml maple syrup
the water from 1 × 400g tin
    of chickpeas (not the
    chickpeas themselves)

FOR THE ICING
400g pure coconut yoghurt
1 tablespoon maple syrup
grated zest of 2 lemons
1 teaspoon ground turmeric

FOR THE LEMON JAM
juice of 5 lemons (about 130ml)
150ml maple syrup
2 tablespoons arrowroot

TO DECORATE (OPTIONAL)
grated zest of 1 lemon
edible flowers

Preheat the oven to 200°C (fan 180°C). Line two 23cm cake tins with baking parchment.

In a large bowl, mix the ground almonds, flour, bicarb, baking powder and lemon zest, stirring well to remove any lumps. When the mixture is well combined, add the lemon juice, maple syrup and chickpea water and mix again until it comes together to form a batter.

Divide the batter evenly between the lined tins and bake for 20 minutes, until risen and a knife inserted in the centre comes out clean. If not, place back in the oven for 5 minutes. Once ready, remove from the oven and leave the cakes to cool in their tins until they reach room temperature.

For the icing, place the coconut yoghurt in a large bowl and whisk using an electric hand whisk (or use a stand mixer) until it becomes really thick and holds itself in peaks, it will take around 5–10 minutes depending on how powerful your whisk is. It is very important to whisk the yoghurt on its own, before adding the maple syrup. When it's thick, add the syrup, lemon zest and turmeric, and continue whisking for a further minute. If you don't have an electric whisk you can use a balloon whisk – just make sure you whisk long enough to get a good amount of air into the mixture so that it thickens.

Make the lemon jam by placing all of the ingredients in a small saucepan over a medium heat, stirring until the mixture begins to thicken, about 10–15 minutes. Once thick enough to coat the back of your spoon, remove and leave to cool.

Once the cakes are cool, spread the jam over one and sandwich it with the other, then smooth the icing over the top. We like to decorate ours with lemon zest and edible flowers but you can leave yours plain.

TIP
As a lighter, super fruity alternative to the icing, you could make double quantities of the jam and use it to cover the top of the cake.

GATHERINGS AND SUPPER CLUBS

The Deliciously Ella Diary
— *part 6*

In this final chapter I want to delve into our evolution. While most of what we do has remained the same, some elements have evolved and along the way we've had some tough decisions to make. The first moment of that evolution came as we created the initial menu for the first deli, Seymour Place. From the minute we started work on the menu we realised we had a real dilemma: I ate an entirely plant-based diet and had shared recipes that fitted that brief, but Matt ate a bit of everything – he loved veggie meals, but he definitely enjoyed eating meat too. We debated it heavily but based our final decision on two points. Firstly, the whole premise behind the deli was our ambition to create somewhere that worked for both of us, on the assumption that it wasn't just us that argued about the choice between dining at raw vegan restaurants and 'normal' restaurants where the plant-based option can be pretty uninspiring. Secondly, and most importantly, we wanted our offering to appeal to everyone – no matter what they ate – so that we could use it to showcase veggie food and hopefully shift some of the negative preconceptions that people had around vegan food. My own experience had shown my friends and family to be very sceptical of vegan food initially, but they were instantly more open-minded towards it when they had something else as a side. They'd then try the meal and discover that the plant-based elements were actually incredibly delicious and, over time, had a change of heart. We thought the same approach would work well at the deli and so decided to offer organic chicken and salmon as side options, with the rest of the menu remaining totally plant-based.

I was pretty nervous about sharing our decision online prior to opening, as I knew it was controversial, but the reaction from some was more intense than I had expected. On the one hand, the majority of our readers were massively supportive of what we were doing – many weren't plant-based, and of those that were, many also struggled with hesitant friends and family so they loved the inclusive approach. On the other hand, we had a handful of very angry people who sent us hate mail, telling us that we'd sold out and had no ethics, and two commenters even went as far as to ask how we'd feel if they ate our dog! It was a tough week, and Matt and I were sad to see that our aim at inclusivity had been met with such a negative reaction from some – after all, wasn't it better to get more people trying elements of vegan food, than not at all?

We continued to serve the organic chicken and salmon as sides for the first year, which did exactly what we thought it would – it brought people who had previously been apprehensive of what we were doing through the door. Awareness of plant-based eating was simultaneously growing rapidly and we found that by mid-2017, about 18 months after opening, it had become mainstream enough that we could take the protein sides off the menu, and our menu has been totally plant-based ever since, which is something I'm very proud of. We still believe it was the right decision initially and I'm glad we weathered the storm. As terrifying as it can be, I'm grateful that we have such a large audience to answer to – I know it keeps us in check, ensures we carefully consider every decision we make and ultimately pushes us to do better in every way.

WE WANTED THE DELI'S OFFERING TO APPEAL TO EVERYONE – TO SHOWCASE VEGGIE FOOD AND HOPEFULLY SHIFT SOME OF THE NEGATIVE PRECONCEPTIONS AROUND VEGAN FOOD

We've also made additions to our recipes and our menu, introducing some new grains and flours – like spelt and rye, as well as artisanal sourdough breads. This has taken Deliciously Ella away from being totally gluten-free, as again we wanted the menu to be reflective of what everyone wanted and I've found myself really enjoying experimenting with these ingredients too.

ALL OF OUR DECISIONS
HAVE BEEN LED
BY OUR COMMUNITY,
AND WE WANT
TO ENSURE THAT
EVERY INTERACTION
OUR READERS
AND FOLLOWERS HAVE
WITH US IS THE
BEST IT CAN BE

All of our decisions have been led by our community, and being a community-led company is something that we all really treasure. In the spirit of this we want to ensure that every interaction our readers and followers have with Deliciously Ella is the best it can be. This is why we eventually came to the conclusion that having just one deli would allow us to keep it more special and ensure that everyone has the best possible experience. It also gives us more flexibility on the menu, allowing us to add more specials and follow the seasons more closely, as any changes can be implemented so much quicker.

When we opened Seymour Place we very quickly realised that it was too small and the shape didn't quite work. It was pinched by the tills, had limited seating and a tiny kitchen. This led us to open Weighhouse Street, which was much more accessible, much bigger, and offers a far superior customer experience. Ultimately it made little sense to have two spaces so close to each other and we wanted to be able to focus all our attention on Weighhouse Street, doing all of our special events there, from afternoon teas to workshops, launches and gatherings. As a result we made the very difficult decision to shut Seymour Place and Herne Hill.

It was a decision led mainly by Matt, but after talking me through his logic I was regrettably fully supportive of the decision. It was a sad, wet day in early March that we closed Seymour Place and Herne Hill and for a few days we wondered whether we'd done the right thing. But looking back, it is one of the best decisions that we've made. I love that having a smaller team means we can have a closer relationship with everyone, that we can do more special events and menu items, and that we can ensure all of our customers are looked after in the best possible way. We stop by Weighhouse Street almost every morning and it really feels like our second home, it's where everything we do originates and I hope it will continue to be our community hub for years to come.

Our aim has always been to take simple things and transform them into something special, adding a little magic to a carrot or a cucumber, and I hope that is what you will find as you cook your way through

this book. Our team at the deli has been working hard on making vegetables the hero of every meal and allowing them to sit pride of place in the centre of any plate – no more boiled sprouts and broccoli!

I've really enjoyed working as part of the group on the deli menu. It's inspiring to have so many talented people to bounce ideas around with, and the input from our customers and readers has been invaluable too. We've definitely had a few items that we've added to the menu thinking that they were brilliant, only to find that they weren't at all what our customers wanted, so we've rapidly made some changes. The favourites always revolve around simple deliciousness, with sweet potatoes, broccoli, curries, stews, dhals and brownies being very popular with most of our regulars. I can't

even begin to count the number of requests we've had for the Five-bean chilli with corn bread (see pages 162–65), our Cauliflower and red lentil dhal (see page 181), Fudgy brownies (see page 200), Green Thai curry (see page 174), cakes (see pages 190–95, 208–11 and 215) and Banana breakfast loaf (see page 57), so I hope you all enjoy them.

The recipes in this final chapter are from our events. They're from the occasions when we've got the most complex and ambitious with our cooking and I hope they give you some inspiration too. I adore the Sweetcorn chowder with chilli and coriander (see page 224), Mushroom and cauliflower risotto (see page 241), Chocolate fudge torte with chocolate sauce (see page 242) and, of course, the Sweet potato wedges with spring onions, chilli and tahini drizzle (see page 232). I think these recipes really highlight that there's so much we can do with simple, natural ingredients and if we all cooked things like this, it would be much easier to get our five-a-day. All we need is a shift in mindset, allowing us to see vegetables as something to be excited about rather than just the soggy sides on our plate.

I can't wait to see what you cook – please do share your delicious plant-based creations with us via social media, or email me:

ella@deliciouslyella.com

MANCHESTER FOOD FESTIVAL

SWEETCORN CHOWDER
WITH CHILLI AND CORIANDER

CREAMY ARTICHOKE
AND EDAMAME DIP

BLACK RICE SALAD
WITH PIQUILLO PEPPERS, PISTACHIOS
AND SULTANAS

ROASTED AUBERGINE,
TOMATO AND PESTO SALAD

SWEET POTATO WEDGES
WITH SPRING ONIONS,
CHILLI AND TAHINI DRIZZLE

ALMOND CAKE
WITH MANGO ICING

SWEETCORN CHOWDER WITH CHILLI AND CORIANDER

We've served this creamy chowder at quite a few events and each time I have found myself staring into the pan hoping there are leftovers for me! It's sweet, creamy and quite unlike anything we've ever made before. It may not sound like it will set your world alight, but trust me you have to try this one. It's phenomenal served with our Fig compote (see page 264).

SERVES 4

500g tinned sweetcorn
    (drained weight)
olive oil
1 onion, chopped
1 garlic clove, chopped
pinch of chilli flakes
1 tablespoon vegetable
    bouillon powder or
    1 vegetable stock cube
juice of 1 lemon
1 × 400g tin of coconut milk
salt and pepper

TO SERVE
100g plain yoghurt (we use
    a pure coconut yoghurt)
handful of coriander leaves,
    chopped

Preheat the oven to 220°C (fan 200°C).

Place the sweetcorn in a large baking tray and drizzle with olive oil. Toss with some salt and pepper and place in the oven for 15–20 minutes, until golden.

Meanwhile, put the onions and garlic into a large saucepan, with a drizzle of olive oil, some salt and pepper and cook gently for 10–15 minutes, or until soft. Add the golden corn to the pan and cook for a further 20 minutes, stirring occasionally to ensure it doesn't stick to the bottom of the pan.

After 20 minutes add the chilli flakes, bouillon powder (or stock cube), lemon juice and coconut milk. Bring to the boil, before reducing the heat and leaving to simmer for 10–15 minutes. Once the kernels feel soft, remove the from the heat and blitz using a hand blender.

Spoon the chowder into bowls and serve with a dollop of yoghurt and some coriander sprinkled on top.

TIP
Bake exta corn kernels to use as the garnish; they look beautiful.

CREAMY ARTICHOKE AND EDAMAME DIP

This dip works beautifully served with the array of dishes in this menu, but I'd advise making extra so that you can enjoy more of it throughout the week. It's delicious spread on rye toast, as a dip for some carrot sticks or simply eaten with a spoon, which seems to be what I tend to do most of the time.

**MAKES 1 BIG BOWL
(ENOUGH TO SERVE 4)**

150g frozen edamame beans, plus extra to garnish
160g artichokes from a jar (drained weight)
1 × 400g tin of butter beans, plus the water from the tin
1 tablespoon smooth almond butter
1 teaspoon lemon juice
1 garlic clove, ideally roasted (see page 35), or 1 raw clove, roughly chopped
2 tablespoons tahini
salt and pepper

Blanch the edamame beans in boiling water for 2 minutes, before draining and placing in a food processor with the rest of the ingredients. Pulse until smooth then check the seasoning before transferring to a serving bowl. Serve with the extra edamame beans sprinkled on top.

BLACK RICE SALAD WITH PIQUILLO PEPPERS, PISTACHIOS AND SULTANAS

The mix of vibrant red, green and black in this salad is really beautiful. As well as being a perfect part of a feast with friends, it also makes a really easy desk lunch: just make a big batch for lunch or dinner at the weekend and enjoy the rest cold throughout the week, adding some simple veggies like avocado chunks or cherry tomatoes and basil to mix it up each day.

SERVES 4 AS A SIDE

200g black rice
80g sultanas
70g pistachios, toasted (see page 35) and roughly chopped
175g piquillo peppers from a jar, drained and cut into thin slices, plus 2 tablespoons of the oil
grated zest of 1 orange, plus the juice of ½
25g coriander, roughly chopped
1 tablespoon maple syrup
salt and pepper

Put the rice into a large pan, cover with water, place over a medium heat and bring to the boil. Once boiling, reduce the heat to a simmer and cook for 35–40 minutes, or until cooked to your liking. Drain well and transfer to a large mixing bowl.

In a small bowl, cover the sultanas with boiling water and soak for 5 minutes, then drain and add them to the mixing bowl, along with the rest of the ingredients, seasoning to taste.

Give everything a really good mix before serving.

TIP
This salad is delicious served hot straight from the pan or at room temperature, but it should not be reheated.

ROASTED AUBERGINE, TOMATO AND PESTO SALAD

This salad worked so well as part of our supper club spread – it's light and simple, and at the right time of year the aubergine, tomato and basil all have so much flavour that they really shine through. It's definitely a summer/early autumn recipe, although the pesto is brilliant at any moment and works really well on its own too, so make extra of it and keep it in the freezer for those times you need a speedy pesto pasta supper and don't have time to cook.

SERVES 4 AS A SIDE

2 large aubergines
olive oil
4–5 large vine tomatoes,
    each cut into 6
handful of basil leaves
    (about 5g), to garnish
salt and pepper

FOR THE PESTO
80g basil leaves
1 red chilli, deseeded
    and chopped
2 garlic cloves, ideally roasted
    (see page 35), or 2 raw
    cloves, roughly chopped
4 sun-dried tomatoes
    from a jar (optional)
150ml olive oil

Preheat the oven to 220°C (fan 200°C).

Slice each aubergine in half crossways, then cut each half into four pieces so you have eight wedges in total, then place these in a large baking tray with a drizzle of olive oil and some salt and pepper, and roast in the oven for 30 minutes.

After 30 minutes, add the tomatoes to the tray and cook for a further 10 minutes.

While the vegetables cook, make the pesto by placing all of the ingredients in a food processor and pulsing until smooth. Season to taste.

Once the vegetables are cooked, remove them from the oven and place in a serving dish, top with spoonfuls of the pesto and garnish with the basil leaves before serving.

TIP
This salad is best served warm, straight from the oven, but is also delicious the next day once the pesto has really infused the vegetables with flavour.

SWEET POTATO WEDGES WITH SPRING ONIONS, CHILLI AND TAHINI DRIZZLE

Sweet potatoes are one of the most popular ingredients we cook with. These sweet potatoes are simple, they're just roasted with olive oil, salt and pepper until sweet and squidgy on the inside and golden on the outside, but then we toss them in a tahini lemon dressing and sprinkle them with chilli, coriander and slices of spring onion. These will be a hit with all your guests, and again the leftovers are perfect for speedy weeknight suppers and packed lunches.

SERVES 4 AS A SIDE

FOR THE WEDGES
2 sweet potatoes
olive oil
1 red chilli, finely chopped
2 spring onions, finely sliced
1 bunch of coriander,
    roughly chopped
salt and pepper

FOR THE DRESSING
3 tablespoons tahini
1 tablespoon lemon juice
2 tablespoons olive oil
pinch of sea salt flakes

Preheat the oven to 240°C (fan 220°C).

Cut the sweet potatoes in half widthways and then cut each half into 8 wedges. Transfer to a large baking tray or roasting tin, drizzle with olive oil, then toss with some salt and pepper, and roast in the oven for 40–45 minutes until soft on the inside and golden on the outside. Once cooked, remove from the oven, toss in the olive oil left in the tray and transfer to a serving platter.

Make the dressing by placing all of the ingredients in a small bowl and whisking until combined.

Drizzle the dressing over the sweet potato wedges, and sprinkle with the chilli, spring onion and coriander before serving.

ALMOND CAKE WITH MANGO ICING

If you're looking for a summery cake this is the one. It's the sponge from our Almond Victoria cake on page 190, topped with a mango icing and chunks of fresh mango on the top. It's sweet and light and the yellow top looks gorgeous.

SERVES 12

300g ground almonds
240g buckwheat flour
1 tablespoon bicarbonate of soda
pinch of sea salt flakes
440ml maple syrup
100ml almond milk
the water from 1 × 400g tin
    of chickpeas (not the
    chickpeas themselves)

FOR THE MANGO ICING
100g dried mango
800g pure coconut yoghurt
2 tablespoons maple syrup

TO DECORATE (OPTIONAL)
12 slices of fresh mango

Preheat the oven to 200°C (fan 180°C). Line two 23cm cake tins with baking parchment.

In a large bowl, mix the ground almonds, buckwheat flour, bicarb and salt, stirring well to remove any lumps. Add the maple syrup, almond milk and chickpea water and mix again until it comes together to form a smooth batter. Pour equal amounts of the batter into the lined tins and bake for 20 minutes, until well risen and a knife inserted in the centre comes out clean – if it doesn't, place the tins back in the oven for 5 minutes. Once ready, remove the cakes from the oven and leave to cool in their tins until room temperature, around 30 minutes.

While the cakes cool, make the icing. Place the dried mango in a small bowl and cover with boiling water, then leave to soak for 10 minutes. Once soaked, place the mango pieces in a food processor with 2 tablespoons of their soaking water and pulse until smooth – it could take about 5 minutes.

Whisk the coconut yoghurt using an electric whisk – either a stand mixer or a hand whisk – until it becomes really thick. It's important to whisk the yoghurt on its own, before adding the maple syrup. Once it feels very thick and holds its shape, add the syrup and mango purée and continue whisking for a further minute. If you don't have an electric whisk you can use a balloon whisk – just make sure you whisk long enough to get a good amount of air into the mix.

Once the cakes are cool, spoon half of the icing over one and sandwich with the other. Smooth the rest of the icing over the top. We like adding fresh pieces of mango on top to decorate.

TIP
The leftover water from soaking the dried mango is absolutely delicious to enjoy on its own as a sweet mango juice.

HELP REFUGEES
CHARITY DINNER

SLOW-ROASTED CARROT
AND SWEDE SOUP
WITH TOASTED HAZELNUTS

MUSHROOM AND CAULIFLOWER
RISOTTO

CHOCOLATE FUDGE TORTE
WITH
CHOCOLATE SAUCE

SLOW-ROASTED CARROT AND SWEDE SOUP WITH TOASTED HAZELNUTS

We created this menu for a Help Refugees fundraiser that we catered for and I think most guests were a little nervous about the concept of a vegan dinner, but every plate was licked clean and it ended up being a big success. After hosting quite a few dinners and supper clubs, we've found that soup is always a popular starter. During the colder months of the year it's especially nice to start with something really warming and this slow-roasted soup with toasted hazelnuts has been one of our most popular.

SERVES 4

1 onion, chopped into pieces
    no larger than 0.5cm
2 garlic cloves, chopped
olive oil
5 large carrots, peeled and sliced
    no thicker than 0.5cm
½ large swede, peeled and
    chopped into pieces no larger
    than 0.5cm
1 teaspoon ground cumin
2 tablespoons vegetable
    boullion powder or
    1 vegetable stock cube
salt and pepper

TO SERVE
handful of hazelnuts,
    toasted (see page 35) and
    roughly chopped
pinch of chilli flakes

Place a pan over a medium heat and add the onion, garlic, a drizzle of olive oil and a pinch of salt and pepper. Cook until soft, about 5–10 minutes. Add the carrots, swede and cumin and cook for another 10–15 minutes, until the carrots begin to soften.

Cover the vegetables with boiling water and add the bouillon powder (or stock cube), then simmer for 45–50 minutes until all of the vegetables are really soft.

Once soft, remove from the heat and blend until smooth. Serve in bowls, garnished with toasted hazelnuts, a pinch of chilli flakes and a drizzle of olive oil.

MUSHROOM AND CAULIFLOWER RISOTTO

When we're catering for guests who may be a little sceptical of a vegan meal we tend to go with dishes that feel familiar and accessible, like a risotto. Here we swapped the traditional butter and cheese for almond milk and nutritional yeast, which I know sounds weird but it works. Cooking the rice in almond milk makes it super creamy and I really recommend trying it in all your risottos, if you're wanting to make them plant-based.

SERVES 4

½ medium butternut squash, peeled, deseeded and cut into cubes no larger than 1cm
olive oil
25g dried porcini mushrooms (or any other dried mushrooms you can find)
400ml boiling water
1 large onion, chopped into pieces no larger than 0.5cm
2 garlic cloves, chopped
2 celery stalks, chopped into pieces no larger than 0.5cm
200g chestnut mushrooms, thinly sliced
1 teaspoon dried rosemary
250g Arborio rice
1 mushroom stock cube or 1 tablespoon vegetable bouillon powder
1–2 tablespoons nutritional yeast
½ cauliflower head, grated or processed using a food processor into a breadcrumb texture
600ml almond milk, plus a little extra if necessary
salt and pepper
handful of parsley, roughly chopped, or micro herbs, to serve

Preheat the oven to 200°C (fan 180°C).

Place the butternut squash in a baking tray with a drizzle of olive oil and a sprinkle of salt and roast in the oven for 35–40 minutes, until soft.

Soak the dried mushrooms in the boiling water for 15–20 minutes, until soft, then drain, reserving the soaking liquid.

Place a deep pan over a medium heat and add about a tablespoon of olive oil. Once the oil is warm, add the onion, garlic, celery and some salt and pepper and cook for 10 minutes, until soft.

Add the chestnut mushrooms and rosemary and cook for 2 minutes before adding the rice. Let this mix with the veg for 30 seconds or so, before adding the stock cube (or bouillon powder), nutritional yeast, soaked mushrooms and cauliflower. Add about 200ml of the almond milk and 200ml of the reserved mushroom water. Bring to the boil, before reducing to a low–medium heat and leaving it to simmer for 15 minutes, adding the rest of the almond milk and mushroom water slowly, and stirring every few minutes to help make it creamy and ensure it doesn't stick to the bottom of the pan.

Once the squash is ready, add it to the risotto and cook for a further 5–10 minutes, adding more almond milk a splash at a time, if needed, until the rice is cooked through and the risotto is thick and creamy. Serve with a sprinkle of parsley or micro herbs.

TIP
To make this dish an even simpler one-pot wonder you can leave out the butternut squash and stir in some spinach instead.

CHOCOLATE FUDGE TORTE WITH CHOCOLATE SAUCE

I ate so many pieces of this torte while we were testing the recipe! It's rich, indulgent and chocolatey with a lovely mix of ground almonds, maple and dates.

SERVES 12

FOR THE CHOCOLATE TORTE
300g ground almonds
150g buckwheat flour
50g cacao powder
50g coconut sugar
pinch of sea salt
200ml maple syrup
100ml date syrup
200ml almond milk
the water from 1 × 400g tin
    of chickpeas (not the
    chickpeas themselves)

FOR THE CHOCOLATE SAUCE
200g pitted dates
600ml almond milk
4 tablespoons cacao powder
1 tablespoon coconut oil
pinch of sea salt

TO SERVE (OPTIONAL)
20g freeze-dried raspberries,
    crushed

Preheat the oven to 200°C (fan 180°C). Line a 25 × 18cm deep baking tray with baking parchment.

In a large bowl, mix together the ground almonds, buckwheat flour, cacao powder, coconut sugar and salt, stirring well to remove any lumps. When the mixture is well combined, add the maple syrup, date syrup, almond milk and chickpea water and mix until it comes together to form a smooth mixture.

Pour the mixture into the lined tray and bake for 20–25 minutes, until cooked through but still a little fudgy. Once cooked, remove from the oven and leave to cool in the tray until room temperature, around 30 minutes.

Make the chocolate sauce by placing the dates in a pan over a medium heat and covering them with the almond milk. Cook for about 15–20 minutes, stirring occasionally, until a paste has formed. Add the cacao powder, coconut oil and salt and stir until combined, adding a little more almond milk if it becomes too thick. Once a thick paste has formed, remove from the heat and leave to cool. Once cool, transfer to a food processor and pulse until smooth.

When the torte has cooled, gently lift it out of the baking tray and cut into rectangles, about 3 × 10cm. Serve each piece of torte with a dollop of the chocolate sauce – you can use the back of your spoon to brush it across the plate for a fancy effect. Sprinkle with a handful of freeze-dried raspberries, if using, before serving.

TIPS
This torte is delicious served with any kind of berry-based yoghurt or ice cream.

You can store the leftover torte in an airtight container in the fridge for up to a week.

WILDERNESS 2017

ROASTED VEGETABLE SALAD WITH
HAZELNUT DRESSING

ROSEMARY BISCUITS
WITH AUBERGINE PURÉE AND
ROASTED VEGETABLES

SEARED POLENTA WITH
SHAVED FENNEL SALAD

LEMON TART WITH
WHIPPED YOGHURT, LEMON GLAZE
AND BERRY COMPOTE

ROASTED VEGETABLE SALAD WITH HAZELNUT DRESSING

This is a lovely simple starter with sweet roasted onions, butternut squash, courgettes and red chillies tossed with an almond butter dressing. Perfect for warm summer nights, which it was when we served it at Wilderness.

**SERVES 8 AS
A SMALL STARTER
OR SIDE**

4 red onions, sliced into
    eight wedges
2 butternut squash, sliced
    into wedges
olive oil
4 courgettes, cut into
    5 circle pieces
4 red chillies, deseeded and sliced
100g blanched hazelnuts,
    toasted (see page 35)
    and roughly chopped
salt and pepper

FOR THE DRESSING
8 tablespoons olive oil
2 tablespoons apple cider vinegar
1 tablespoon almond butter
pinch of sea salt flakes

Preheat the oven to 220°C (fan 200°C).

Place the onion and squash in a baking tray, drizzle with olive oil and mix with salt and pepper. Roast in the oven for 30 minutes until golden. Once these have been in the oven for 30 minutes, add the courgettes and cook for a further 15–20 minutes until golden.

While the vegetables are in the oven, make the dressing by placing the oil, vinegar, almond butter and salt in a bowl and whisking with a fork until smooth.

Once the vegetables have cooked, transfer them to a serving dish and drizzle the dressing over the top, then sprinkle with the chopped hazelnuts before serving.

ROSEMARY BISCUITS WITH AUBERGINE PURÉE AND ROASTED VEGETABLES

This dish is absolutely delicious as part of a dinner spread, but I think it's the rosemary biscuits that are the true star and one of the hidden gems in this book. Even if you're not going to try the whole dish, do make the biscuits. They're brilliant as simple little canapés if you cut them into smaller circles or simply as savoury snacks – our whole office has become addicted to them as afternoon nibbles!

MAKES 8

FOR THE ROSEMARY BISCUITS
250g ground almonds
100ml almond milk
2 tablespoons brown rice flour, plus extra to dust
1 tablespoon coconut oil
2 teaspoons dried rosemary
pinch of salt

FOR THE AUBERGINE PURÉE
2 large aubergines, halved lengthways
2 tablespoons olive oil
2 tablespoons tahini
2 garlic cloves, chopped
juice of 1 lemon
1 tablespoon date syrup
salt and pepper

FOR THE ROASTED VEGETABLE TOPPING
100g Tenderstem broccoli
200g chestnut mushrooms, halved
2 large vine tomatoes, cut into quarters
olive oil
dried chilli flakes, to serve

Preheat the oven to 220°C (fan 200°C).

Start by making the aubergine purée and roasted vegetable topping. Place the aubergines on a baking tray with a tablespoon of olive oil, and roast in the oven for 30 minutes. After 30 minutes, put the broccoli, mushrooms and tomatoes into a separate baking tray, drizzle with olive oil, toss with salt and pepper and roast in the oven for 10 minutes. Once cooked, remove from the oven and leave to one side until ready to use. When the aubergines are golden and cooked through, remove from the oven and scrape the flesh into a food processor. Add the remaining tablespoon of olive oil and the rest of the purée ingredients and pulse until a smooth paste forms.

Make the biscuits by placing all of the ingredients in a food processor and pulsing until well combined. Once combined, roll into a large ball and chill in the fridge for 30 minutes to firm up. Turn the oven down to 200°C (fan 180°C) and line a baking tray with baking parchment.

Remove the firm dough from the fridge and roll it out on a floured work surface until 1cm thick. Cut out circles of dough – the size you want your biscuits to be (we make ours about 12cm) – and transfer them to the lined tray, then place in the oven for 20–25 minutes, watching them carefully until golden. To serve, spoon a tablespoon of the aubergine purée on to each biscuit, top with the roasted vegetables and sprinkle with a pinch of chilli flakes.

TIP

To serve the biscuits as canapés; cut smaller discs of the dough and top them with anything you like – the pesto on page 231 is delicious.

SEARED POLENTA WITH SHAVED FENNEL SALAD

I absolutely love polenta and it's always been popular at our events too. We've made this recipe for a few supper clubs we've held at the deli and the plates have always come back clean. Because it has quite a plain flavour, the polenta is also very versatile, so you can pretty much top it as you like – we've cut it into little cubes and topped these with a cashew sweet potato purée or a basil pesto to serve as canapés, which were amazing.

MAKES 12

FOR THE POLENTA
750ml almond milk
120g polenta
1 tablespoon olive oil
1 teaspoon dried rosemary
1 teaspoon nutritional yeast
    (optional, but it adds
    a great flavour)
salt

FOR THE TOMATO RELISH
250g plum tomatoes
150g sun-dried tomatoes (drained
    weight), plus 2 tablespoons
    of oil from the jar
20g basil, plus a few small leaves
    to garnish
1 garlic clove, roasted (see page 35)
    and roughly chopped
handful of almonds (about 20g,
    optional)
2 tablespoons tomato purée
1 red chilli, deseeded and
    roughly chopped
salt and pepper

FOR THE FENNEL SALAD
1 fennel bulb, finely sliced (you can
    use a mandolin if you have one,
    if not just slice really thinly
    using a sharp knife)
200g radishes, finely sliced
2 tablespoons apple cider vinegar
2 tablespoons maple syrup
1 tablespoon olive oil
1 tablespoon lemon juice
1 tablespoon dried rosemary

Line a deep 18cm × 25cm baking tray with baking parchment.

For the polenta, place the almond milk and a generous sprinkling of salt in a pan over a medium heat and bring to the boil. Gradually stir in the polenta, ensuring there are no lumps. Once it's starting to thicken turn the heat down. Cook the polenta over a low heat for about 20 minutes, stirring frequently to keep it creamy and ensure it doesn't stick to the bottom of the pan. Once the polenta is thick and combined, remove from the heat, add 1 tablespoon of the olive oil, the rosemary and nutritional yeast, then taste to see whether the salt levels are right – adjust if you need to. Pour the polenta into the baking tray and leave to set in the fridge for 1–2 hours.

Preheat the oven to 220°C (fan 200°C).

Bake the polenta in the oven for 15 minutes. Once cooked, remove and leave to cool – this allows it to firm up so that it crisps better when fried.

While the polenta is cooking, make the tomato relish by placing all of the ingredients in a food processor and pulsing until smooth.

Place the fennel and radishes in a large mixing bowl with the rest of the salad ingredients, giving everything a really good mix.

To serve, cut the polenta into 12 thick slices (you could cut bigger slices to make 8 pieces if you prefer). Place a pan over a medium heat and add a drizzle of olive oil. Once warm, fry the polenta slices on each side for 2 minutes, until golden. Place each slice on to a plate, top with tomato relish, a tablespoon of fennel and radish salad and garnish with a few basil leaves. Any leftover polenta can be stored in an airtight container in the fridge for up to 2 days.

LEMON TART WITH WHIPPED YOGHURT, LEMON GLAZE AND BERRY COMPOTE

The bases for these lemon tarts are brilliant, they're really easy to make and look really fancy when you add the whipped yoghurt, berry compote and lemon glaze. You can mix these up a little too, adding other flavours to the tart – it's lovely adding a little orange zest to the lemon mix or take the lemon out and use cinnamon and ginger instead.

MAKES 12

FOR THE BASE
250g ground almonds
100ml maple syrup
grated zest and juice
    of 1 lemon
2 tablespoons brown rice flour
1 tablespoon coconut oil,
    melted

FOR THE BERRY COMPOTE
400g frozen or fresh
    mixed berries
3 tablespoons maple syrup
2 tablespoons chia seeds

FOR THE WHIPPED YOGHURT
400g pure coconut yoghurt
50ml maple syrup

FOR THE LEMON GLAZE
juice of 5 large lemons
150ml maple syrup
2 level tablespoons arrowroot

TO SERVE (OPTIONAL)
handful of freeze-dried
    raspberries
handful of micro basil

Preheat the oven to 200°C (fan 180°C). Line a 18cm × 25cm baking tray with baking parchment.

Put all of the base ingredients into a bowl and mix until well combined. Once combined, spoon the mixture into the lined tray, pressing down with your hands to even out. Bake in the oven for 20–25 minutes until golden, then remove and leave to cool to room temperature in the tray, around 20 minutes.

To make the berry compote, place the berries and maple syrup in a small saucepan over a medium–low heat and cook for 5–10 minutes, until the berries are soft. Once soft, remove the pan from the heat and mash the berries using the back of a fork or potato masher, then add the chia seeds, return the pan to the heat and cook for a further 15 minutes. Remove and leave to cool to room temperature.

Make the whipped yoghurt by placing the coconut yoghurt in a large bowl (or stand mixer) and whisk using an electric whisk until it becomes really thick, around 5–10 minutes – it's really important to mix the coconut yoghurt on its own first, before adding the maple syrup. Once thick, add the syrup and continue whisking for a further minute. If you don't have an electric whisk you can use a balloon whisk – just make sure you whisk long enough to get a good amount of air and thickness into the mixture, about 10–15 minutes.

recipe continues overleaf

Make the lemon glaze by placing all of the ingredients in a small pan set over a medium heat and stir until it begins to thicken, about 10–15 minutes. Once thick enough to coat the back of your spoon, remove and leave to cool to room temperature, about 10 minutes.

Once all of the elements are made and cool you are ready to assemble your tarts. Spoon all of the lemon glaze on to the tart base, smoothing it all over with a spoon, then cut the base into rectangles (about 3 × 10cm) and place each on to a plate. Top with dollops of the whipped yoghurt (or see tip below) and dollops of the berry compote. We also like to sprinkle some freeze-dried raspberries and micro basil over the top, but you don't need to.

TIPS

We suggest cutting the base of the tart into 12 pieces, but you could cut bigger slices to make 8 pieces if you prefer. Alternatively, you can store the extra pieces in an airtight container in the fridge for up to 5 days.

If you have a piping bag you can pipe the yoghurt on for a smoother finish.

For our event, we used a lemon curd instead of the glaze, which is what you can see in the image, but we felt the glaze was a more simple and delicious version for you to make at home. If you wanted to recreate the tart we made you could make or buy a thick lemon curd and add dollops of it to the tarts along with the berry compote and whipped yoghurt.

Deliciously Ella
WILDERNESS BANQUET
— Menu —

Five Bean
Chilli with
crunchy slaw

HERNE HILL
SUPPER CLUB

WARM ALMOND AND BEETROOT SOUP

SWEETCORN CHOWDER
WITH FIG COMPOTE

TOMATO AND BASIL CARPACCIO

GARLICKY FRENCH BEANS WITH
WHOLEGRAIN MUSTARD AND TRUFFLE

PULLED AUBERGINE SLIDERS

CHOCOLATE AND COCONUT
TRUFFLES

WARM ALMOND AND BEETROOT SOUP

We've had consistently mixed feedback about beetroot but this soup is my favourite way to use it. The soup went down so well at our supper club that even if you're a beetroot sceptic I'm hoping this might encourage you to give it a try. The almond butter and almond milk make the soup really creamy, but they also mellow the beetroot flavour. The toasted almonds on the top add a great crunch.

SERVES 4

1 onion, roughly chopped
2 garlic cloves, roughly chopped
olive oil
4 cooked beetroots, roughly chopped
pinch of dried chilli flakes
1 tablespoon vegetable bouillon powder or 1 vegetable stock cube
1 tablespoon lemon juice
1 tablespoon maple syrup
500ml almond milk
1 teaspoon almond butter
salt and pepper
handful of almonds (about 20g), toasted (see page 35), roughly chopped, to serve
plain yoghurt (we use a pure coconut yoghurt), to serve
handful of coriander sprigs, to serve (optional)

Place the onion and garlic in a large pan over a medium heat, with a drizzle of olive oil and some salt and pepper. Cook for 10–15 minutes, until soft. Add the beetroot and cook for a further 10 minutes, stirring occasionally to ensure it doesn't stick to the bottom of the pan.

Add the chilli flakes, bouillon powder (or stock cube), lemon juice, maple syrup and almond milk. Bring to the boil, before lowering the heat and leaving to simmer for 35–40 minutes, until the beetroot is soft. Once soft, remove from the heat, add the almond butter, and blitz using a hand blender until smooth.

Spoon the soup into small bowls and serve with a sprinkle of chopped almonds, a dollop of yoghurt and some coriander, if using.

TIP
This soup is delicious served warm, or at room temperature, because of its thick consistency. It is very rich so we recommend serving it in small bowls or glasses as a starter.

SWEETCORN CHOWDER
WITH FIG COMPOTE

As this chowder is such a crowd-pleaser we've made it for events many times, but adding the fig compote takes it to another level. You also need to have the compote on its own too, it's the most incredible addition to breakfast – I love it with our Nutty Granola and some coconut yoghurt or spooned on top of porridge, but it's also delicious on oat crackers as an afternoon snack.

SERVES 4

Sweetcorn chowder
 (see page 224)

FOR THE FIG COMPOTE
5 fresh figs
2 tablespoons maple syrup
1 teaspoon lemon juice
pinch of sea salt flakes

To make the compote, simply place all of the ingredients in a small pan over a medium heat and cook until soft, around 15–20 minutes. Once soft, mash everything together using the back of a fork or a potato masher, until it is as chunky or smooth as you like it.

Once cooked, spoon on top of the sweetcorn chowder to serve.

TOMATO AND BASIL CARPACCIO

This is definitely a recipe for the summer when tomatoes are in season and at their ripest. It's so simple but together the ingredients are a classic combination and completely delicious – you'll be eating this all summer, with everything! Use a mixture of large yellow, orange and red tomatoes to make it even more stunning.

SERVES 4 AS A SIDE

9 large vine tomatoes, cut into slices no thicker than 0.5cm
2 garlic cloves, finely chopped
2 tablespoons olive oil
handful of basil or micro herbs, finely chopped, plus a few extra leaves to garnish
1 tablespoon balsamic vinegar
large pinch of sea salt flakes
handful of capers (about 20g)
50g vegan cheese (optional; we use Nutcrafter Creamery mozzarella)

Simply place the tomatoes, garlic, olive oil, half of the basil (or micro herbs), balsamic vinegar and salt in a large bowl and mix well.

Layer the tomatoes on top of each other on a large serving plate, starting around the outside and circling inwards. Garnish with the capers, dots of vegan cheese, if using, and the remaining basil (or micro herbs) before serving.

TIP
For the supper club we lightly fried our capers in olive oil to make them extra crispy, but you don't need to do this if you don't want to.

GARLICKY FRENCH BEANS WITH WHOLEGRAIN MUSTARD AND TRUFFLE

This is up there with the fanciest dishes we've ever made, but before you panic, you can skip the truffle – it's just an extra we added for some of our more gourmet events, and this salad is still heavenly without it. This recipe works brilliantly as part of a salad spread or on its own.

SERVES 4 AS A SIDE

200g green beans, washed
1 tablespoon olive oil
3 garlic cloves, peeled and roughly chopped
2 tablespoons wholegrain mustard
10g black truffle from a jar, thinly sliced
1 tablespoon maple syrup
pinch of sea salt flakes

Place a pan of water over a medium heat and bring to the boil. Add the beans and cook for 3 minutes, before removing and rinsing with cold water to stop them from cooking further. Drain well and leave to one side.

Place a large pan over a medium heat and add the olive oil. Once warm, add the green beans and garlic and cook for 5–10 minutes, until the beans become crispy. Once cooked, put the beans into a large mixing bowl and add the mustard, truffle, maple syrup and salt flakes. Give everything a really good stir before serving.

PULLED AUBERGINE SLIDERS

I'm really excited about you being able to make these – they're such a fun dish. We make them as mini sliders, which is great as part of a big spread or as a canapé, but you can also make them larger and serve them in big buns as a main. The slider mix tastes really good with brown rice too so any leftover mixture is perfect the following day.

MAKES 10 MINI SLIDERS

2 aubergines
olive oil
1 onion, chopped
2 garlic cloves, chopped
1 teaspoon ground cumin
2 tablespoons tomato purée
1 tablespoon almond butter
½ × 400g tin of chopped
    tomatoes
pinch of dried chilli flakes
juice of ½ lemon
salt and pepper

TO SERVE
10 mini burger buns (optional)
handful of micro coriander
    (optional)
pinch of dried chilli flakes

Preheat the oven to 220°C (fan 200°C).

Place the aubergines in a deep baking tray and roast in the oven for 45 minutes, until soft.

While the aubergines are cooking, make the sauce by placing a pan over a medium heat, with a drizzle of olive oil. Add the onion, garlic and cumin and cook for 10 minutes, until soft. Add the tomato purée, almond butter, chopped tomatoes, chilli flakes, lemon juice, and some salt and pepper, and cook for a further 10 minutes, stirring occasionally to make sure nothings sticks to the bottom of the pan.

Once the aubergines are cooked, cut them in half and use a fork to scrape the flesh into long strands. Add the strands of aubergine to the sauce and stir through.

Once you are ready to serve, place a tablespoon of the pulled aubergine mixture inside each mini burger bun, if using, top with the micro coriander, if using, and sprinkle with a pinch of chilli flakes.

CHOCOLATE AND COCONUT TRUFFLES

We've served these at almost all of our dinner events. They're a nice small bite of sweetness to end a meal for those who don't love a big dessert or a nice extra one for those that really love it (like me!). These are great little snacks too, perfect as mid-afternoon pick-me-ups.

MAKES 6

50g desiccated coconut
12 Medjool dates, pitted
    and chopped
2 tablespoons coconut milk
    (from a carton)
1 teaspoon coconut oil
3 tablespoons raw cacao powder

Place the desiccated coconut in a baking tray lined with baking parchment and set to one side.

Put the remaining ingredients into a food processor and pulse until well combined. Once everything has come together, spoon out tablespoons of the mixture and use your hands to roll them into balls.

Roll the balls in the desiccated coconut until well coated then place on a clean baking sheet or dish. Place the baking sheet in the fridge to chill for at least 30 minutes before serving.

C

Acknowledgements

With each book the list of thank yous gets longer and my sense of gratitude gets bigger.

First and foremost I have to thank our community. What started as a little group of us on deliciouslyella.com and then on Instagram has grown beyond my wildest dreams. The encouragement and support that you've all shown us is incredible. It's given me the courage to chase every dream and it's picked us up after every bump in the road. None of what we've created would exist without you, and I just hope that cooking these recipes will make you as happy as you make us.

I have such deep gratitude to the Deliciously Ella team: they're the most talented group of people I've met and I've learnt so much from them. A special thank you to Lily who worked tirelessly on testing and retesting these recipes to ensure that everything was perfect for you; to Louise for her stunning work on our designs; to Holly for looking after the deli so brilliantly from day one; to Dan for trusting us and coming on board to build the products business so expertly; and to Alan, Betty, George, Ed, Vic, Sally, Ian, Holly F, Sophie and Sophie, Andrew and Olivia for bringing Deliciously Ella to life each day.

Thank you to my husband, partner, Deliciously Ella CEO and all-round hero, Matt. He's supported me through every step of this journey and working together has made every element of Deliciously Ella more fun than it would have ever been without him. He's taught me so much, and more than anything has shown me the importance of self-belief and positive thinking.

And finally, thank you to Yellow Kite, WME and the rest of our book team for making The Cookbook so special. To Liz for her never-ending support of Deliciously Ella; to Simon, Gordy and Chekka for encouraging and advising us every step of the way; to Louise and Caitriona for all the inspired creativity around our launch; to Imogen for being the most brilliant and patient editor; to Nassima for the completely stunning photography; to Tamara and Cynthia for the fantastic food and prop styling; and to Sandra for bringing each page together.

First published in Great Britain in 2018 by Yellow Kite Books
An Imprint of Hodder & Stoughton
An Hachette UK company

3

Publisher: Liz Gough
Editor: Imogen Fortes
Design: Sandra Zellmer
Cover design: Deliciously Ella
Photography: Nassima Rothacker and Sophia Spring
Food Styling: Tamara Vos
Prop Styling: Cynthia Blackett
Hair and make-up: Khandiz Joni
Senior Production Controller: Susan Spratt

Colour origination by Born Group
Printed and bound by Firmengruppe APPL, aprinta druck, Wemding, Germany

Yellow Kite
Hodder & Stoughton Ltd
Carmelite House
50 Victoria Embankment
London EC4Y 0DZ

www.yellowkitebooks.co.uk
www.hodder.co.uk

CONVERSION TABLE

All equivalents are rounded, for practical convenience.

OVEN TEMPERATURES

Celsius	Fahrenheit
140	275
150	300
160	325
180	350
190	375
200	400
220	425
230	450
240	465

WEIGHT

25g	1 oz
50g	2 oz
100g	3½ oz
150g	5 oz
200g	7 oz
250g	9 oz
300g	10 oz
400g	14 oz
500g	1 lb 2 oz
1kg	2¼ lb

VOLUME (LIQUIDS)

5ml		1 tsp
15ml		1 tbsp
30ml	1 fl oz	⅛ cup
60ml	2 fl oz	¼ cup
75ml		⅓ cup
120ml	4 fl oz	½ cup
150ml	5 fl oz	⅔ cup
175ml		¾ cup
250ml	8 fl oz	1 cup
1 litre	1 quart	4 cups

LENGTH

1cm	½ inch
2.5cm	1 inch
20cm	8 inches
25cm	10 inches
30cm	12 inches

VOLUME (DRY INGREDIENTS – AN APPROXIMATE GUIDE)

rolled oats	1 cup = 100g
fine powders (e.g. flour)	1 cup = 125g
nuts (e.g. almonds)	1 cup = 125g
seeds (e.g. chia)	1 cup = 160g
dried fruit (raisins etc.)	1 cup = 150g
dried legumes (large, e.g. chickpeas)	1 cup = 170g
grains, granular goods and small dried legumes (e.g. rice, quinoa, sugar, lentils)	1 cup = 200g

If you enjoyed cooking from and reading this book, you might be interested in the other Deliciously Ella titles:

Deliciously Ella

Awesome ingredients and incredible food that you and your body will love

Ella Woodward

Deliciously Ella Every Day

Simple recipes and fantastic food for a healthy way of life

Ella Woodward

Deliciously Ella with Friends

Healthy recipes to love, share and enjoy together

Deliciously Ella Smoothies & Juices